S A V E D   B Y   S O U P

SAVED BY Soup

MORE THAN 100 DELICIOUS
LOW-FAT SOUP RECIPES
TO EAT AND ENJOY EVERY DAY

Judith Barrett

PHOTOGRAPHS BY MELANIE ACEVEDO

WILLIAM MORROW AND COMPANY, INC., NEW YORK

Library of Congress Cataloging-in-Publication Data
Barrett, Judith, 1948–
Saved by soup : more than 100 delicious low-fat soup recipes
to eat and enjoy every day / by Judith Barrett. —1st ed.
p. cm.
Includes index.
ISBN 0-688-15300-3
1. Soups. 2. Low-fat diet—Recipes. I. Title.
TX757.B376 1999
641.8'13—dc21   98-6421
CIP

Printed in the United States of America

First Edition

2 3 4 5 6 7 8 9 10

BOOK DESIGN BY OKSANA KUSHNIR

www.williammorrow.com

FOR DAVID, ANNIE, AND RACHEL

ACKNOWLEDGMENTS

▼
▼
▼
▼
▼
▼
▼
▼
▼
▼
▼
▼
▼
▼
▼
▼
▼
▼
▼
▼
▼
▼
▼
▼
▼
▼

A million thanks to all my friends and family. Their encouragement and support have been invaluable.

I am also grateful to Mary Donlon for her help with recipe testing, Debby Jacobs for her copy-editing skills, and Christin Loudon, R.D., for her nutritional expertise. I am particularly indebted to my agent, Doe Coover, for her guidance and friendship, and Pam Hoenig for her editorial wisdom and for seeing this project through.

CONTENTS

*O*f all the foods we eat and enjoy, there is nothing like a bowl of soup to nourish, to comfort, and to satisfy. Nothing warms better on a cold winter day, or refreshes more on a hot summer night. And no prescription could ever heal quite like a bowl of chicken broth.

In addition to its popularity and flexibility, soup, it turns out, is ideal if you're counting calories and grams of fat. When I decided to shed excess pounds that were inching my scale up and my waistband out, I discovered how healthful and diet-friendly good soup can be when it's part of a sensible eating plan.

Once I cut back on the quantities I was eating and the added fat in the food I was preparing, creating a satisfying dinner became a major challenge. It was then that I began eating low-fat soup regularly with lunch and dinner. As a gratifying, hunger-quelling, guilt-free first course, it provided balance and substance to a lean meal. I wasn't leaving the table hungry. Soup—comforting, warming, and filling—saved the day, and me too.

Of course, not just any soup would do. It had to be low in fat and calories for me to be comfortable consuming it. I know too well the way commercial food purveyors cook to make food taste good:

Take-out shops and restaurants pour in oil with abandon and add butter and cream copiously.

In my own kitchen I discovered that all types of soups—thick combinations of vegetables, beans, and grains, vegetable purees, or delicate, broth-based soups—can be created in a low-fat form without compromising either the taste or the texture. That's because the combination of a savory broth and deliciously fresh raw ingredients results in hearty, satisfying, and well-flavored soups. So soup became one of the pillars of my diet, which was actually just a healthful approach to eating. Scientists, nutritionists, and doctors alike agree that a balanced diet low in fat along with a daily regimen of sensible exercise is the best way to live. And low-fat soups can be an ideal, integral part of that approach.

Some of the earliest soups, from ancient Rome, were like a porridge or thick gruel. Eventually it was discovered that broth could be poured over stale bread to make a hearty, nourishing, and cheap meal. The word soup actually comes from the Teutonic word for the slice of bread over which the broth was poured: *sop* and *sup* in old English, *soupe* (in French), *sopa* (in Spanish), and *soep* (in Dutch). Once broth was poured over bread it followed that broth could be poured over grains, legumes, meats, fish, game, and every noodle imaginable.

Now the whole world loves soup. The French have *soupe* and *potage* and the Italians *zuppa* (a thick soup) and *brodo* (broth). Asia has an abundance of soups, from the incredibly simple *miso* and *dashi* (broths) of Japan to the *keng* (a stew of meat and vegetables) of China, and the *pho* (noodle soups) of Vietnam. Russia, Ukraine, and Eastern Europe have *borscht* (always made with beet root, plus other ingredients) and *shchi* (always made with cabbage, plus other ingredients). There is *gazpacho* (made red with tomatoes or white with almonds) in Spain; scores of different *dal shorba* (lentil soups) in India; *tinola* (chicken soup) in the Philippines; *harira* (lamb soup) in Morocco; and *pozole* (hominy soup) in Mexico.

Drawing upon this vast gastronomic diversity and my foundation of culinary interests and work, I have tried to create a variety of recipes that are as delicious as they are healthful, and all very easy to prepare. Low-fat soups to eat and enjoy every day. You too can be *Saved by Soup*.

FAT
FACTS

With so much hysteria these days about fat, it may be surprising to learn in this book of low-fat soups that there is some fat in almost every recipe.

These recipes are consistent with the current nutritional research and thinking with regard to fat and diet. Most nutrition experts recommend reducing fat in the average diet, but they also agree that fat shouldn't be cut out completely. In fact, they say that some fat in the average person's diet is actually beneficial. The specific amount of fat will vary from individual to individual, but it is generally accepted that about 30 percent of the calories in an average person's daily diet should come from fat. According to the Boston University Medical Center, the amount of fat in your daily diet depends on how many calories you take in. For example, a 1,600-calorie-a-day diet should contain approximately 53 grams of fat, while a 2,000-calorie-a-day diet should include 67 grams of fat.

Given that some fat is good for you, which fats are better and which ones should be avoided? In the most general terms, it is the saturated fats that should be avoided and the polyunsaturated and monounsaturated fats that should be preferred, although all types of fat and ultimately the total amount of fat in the diet should be controlled.

Animal fats are saturated fats—butter, chicken fat, and lard—and are generally not considered to be heart-healthy, while liquid vegetable fats—corn oil, safflower oil, sunflower oil, and soybean oil, which are polyunsaturated, and olive oil, canola oil, and peanut oil, which are monounsaturated—are lower in saturated fat and are viewed as easier on your heart. The exceptions are those few vegetable fats, such as palm kernel oil, and coconut oil, which are saturated and considered to be as unhealthful as animal fats. Saturated fats raise blood cholesterol levels more than anything else in the diet.

When it comes to losing weight, I often tell people, fat is fat; most fats are almost the same in terms of calories and total grams of fat. A tablespoon of butter has about 101 calories and a tablespoon of olive oil has about 119 calories. They both have about 12 grams of fat total. Butter, however, has 7 grams of saturated fat while olive oil has only 2 grams of saturated fat. When you switch to olive oil from butter you may be doing your heart a favor but both fats will have the same effect on your waistline.

The Dietary Guidelines for Americans recommend no more than 10 percent of calories from saturated fat. Therefore, everyone should eat less saturated fat. The following is a comparison of 1 tablespoon of each of the fats:

TYPE OF FAT (1 tablespoon)	CALORIES	TOTAL FAT/GRAMS	SAT. FAT/GRAMS (part of total)
Butter	101	11.5	7.2
Olive oil	119	13.5	1.8
Canola oil	120	13.6	1.0
Chicken fat	115	12.8	3.8
Lard	116	12.8	5.1

If losing weight is what you want to do, it's important to reduce the quantity of fat as well as change the type of fat in your diet and in your cooking. But just cutting fat won't necessarily help you to lose weight. You also have to cut calories, and some low-fat food can be highly caloric. However, if your concern about fat is based on health issues other than weight, such as high blood cholesterol or heart disease, then the type of fat counts as much as the quantity.

I have tried to make all the recipes in this book as low in fat and as low in calories as possible without compromising my standards for deliciously flavorful, good-tasting soups prepared with the best, freshest ingredients. I have done this by keeping the added fat in the soup recipes down to a minimum, adding only teaspoons of oil; using homemade defatted broth; adding nonfat yogurt or nonfat sour cream in the recipes calling for those ingredients; cooking with skinless, boneless white meat chicken, low-fat shellfish, white-fleshed fish, and low-fat tofu; and avoiding red meat, meat broth, and meat bones.

The fat and calorie content of the recipes ranges from almost zero to about 3 grams of fat per serving, lower than most commercial soup brands and almost certainly lower than soup you would order in a restaurant. Federal guidelines mandate that foods labeled "low fat" must not have more than 3 grams of fat per serving. "Nonfat," according to the FDA, has less than .5 gram of fat per serving. The serving size of the recipes in this book is a generous ¾ cup but not as weighty as a restaurant portion, which is often more than a cup.

The nutritional information—grams of fat and calories per serving—is listed at the end of each recipe and both have been rounded off. I arrived at the nutritional analysis through several different computer software programs which employ the database from the U.S. Department of Agriculture—the listing of the composition of foods, considered to be the definitive nutritional analysis of foods—as well as data from other sources. According to Dr. Pat Plummer, chairperson of the Department of Family and Consumer Sciences at Framingham State College in Massachusetts, all nutritional information or data—whether of grams of fat, milligrams of sodium or potassium, or calories—is calibrated on an average taken from analyzing a food several times. There is no finite amount of anything in any food—minerals, fat, and calories will vary from carrot to carrot or soup to soup. Therefore, the nutritional analyses provided with these recipes are meant to act as a guide—not as a medical prescription. If you have any concerns regarding your health and these recipes, please consult your doctor.

While these recipes have been created as low fat and low calorie, they are not specifically low-sodium recipes. However, all of the recipes have salt listed as an ingredient with the quantity given as according to taste. Feel free to adjust the quantity of the salt or eliminate it altogether if your diet necessitates it.

SOUP STARTERS: ESSENTIALS FOR MAKING LOW-FAT SOUP

TAKING STOCK

The foundation for all of the recipes in this book is home-made broth that is well seasoned, flavorful, and *defatted*, which is to say as free of fat as is possible to make in your kitchen. All the fat and calorie quantities given in the recipes reflect a defatted, low-fat broth.

To get the most flavor in your broth, whether you are making a robust, roasted vegetable broth or a richly flavored chicken broth, use the freshest and best available ingredients. They will give you a soup base with a deliciously honest, fresh taste.

Then, to make the broth as low in fat as possible, it is necessary to follow a few steps—steps that require extra hours after you've finished cooking the broth, but very little extra work. First, strain the solids from the broth, firmly pressing the cooked ingredients against the strainer to extract as much of the broth as possible. Thoroughly chill the strained broth for at least 8 hours or preferably overnight, which will cause any fat to rise to the surface of the chilled broth and harden. Use a metal spoon to lift and remove as much of the fat as is physically possible. Skimming the fat from the surface of hot soup does not accomplish defatting as thoroughly.

This method will significantly lower the fat content of your broth but it is not possible to completely defat a broth by hand. To make the recipes in this book even lower in fat, you can substitute a nonfat store-bought broth.

If you want to use an instant dry bouillon or canned low-fat broth, be sure to read the nutritional information on the package to choose a brand that's as low in fat as possible. If you are unsure about the fat content of the canned or dried product, you can defat the broth using the same method as described above: Prepare the broth with water (if using bouillon) and chill, or chill the canned broth; remove the hardened fat with a spoon. When I use instant bouillon cubes, I avoid those with an overly strong or particularly salty taste that could overpower the finished soup. In addition, I usually overdilute the cubes to diffuse their distinctive flavor in a ratio of 2.5 to 1.

Following are recipes for broth that can be used in the preparation of the soups in this book. Most of the recipes call for chicken or vegetable broth. In addition, I have included recipes for fish broth and Asian chicken broth, which you will find helpful in the preparation of a selection of the recipes. Homemade broth will usually keep well in the refrigerator for up to five days. You can keep broth frozen for up to three months.

LOW-FAT CHICKEN BROTH

▼ ▼

1 whole chicken (about
   3 pounds) or parts such as
   wings, backs, and necks

1 medium-size onion

4 medium-size carrots,
   cut into 2-inch pieces

4 ribs celery, trimmed and cut
   into 2-inch pieces

1 small bunch fresh parsley,
   rinsed

4 quarts cold water

Salt to taste

This flavorful, basic chicken broth is a good base for most soups. You'll find it has a mild chicken flavor with no other strong defining flavors to compete with the taste of the soup you are preparing.

▼ ▼ ▼

Combine all the ingredients in an 8-quart stockpot and place over high heat. When the liquid comes to a boil, reduce the heat to medium-low, cover the pot, and simmer, skimming the surface occasionally, until the chicken is falling-off-the-bone tender, 1½ to 2 hours. Allow to stand and cool to room temperature.

Strain the broth through a large sieve or colander into a bowl or plastic container. Use a wooden spoon to press the chicken and vegetables against the sieve to extract as much of the broth as possible. (Reserve the chicken and vegetables to eat separately, if desired.) Cover the container and place in the refrigerator until thoroughly chilled and the fat has hardened on the surface, at least 8 hours or preferably overnight. Use a slotted metal spoon or spatula to remove all of the fat from the broth.

Divide the broth into two or three smaller containers and store in the refrigerator for up to five days or freeze for up to three months.

MAKES ABOUT 3 QUARTS ▾ SERVING SIZE 1 CUP
Nutritional information
18 calories ▾ 0.7 grams of fat

▼ ▼

1 whole chicken (about 3 pounds) or parts such as wings, backs, and necks

One 2-inch piece fresh gingerroot, sliced into 2 or 3 pieces

2 tablespoons sake (Japanese rice wine)

Salt to taste

*A*sian seasonings give this light chicken broth its distinctive character. Use it for the Asian-inspired soup recipes in the chapter Far Eastern Flavors. I like to keep this broth simple, but you can add flavorings such as lemongrass and cilantro for a more complex taste.

▼ ▼ ▼

Combine all the ingredients in an 8-quart stockpot over high heat. When the water boils, reduce the heat to medium-low, cover the pot, and simmer, skimming the surface occasionally, until the chicken is falling-off-the-bone tender, 1½ to 2 hours. Allow to stand and cool to room temperature.

Strain the broth through a large sieve or colander into a bowl or plastic container. Use a wooden spoon to press the chicken against the sieve to extract as much of the broth as possible. (Reserve the chicken to eat separately, if desired.) Cover the container and place in the refrigerator until thoroughly chilled and the fat has hardened on the surface of the broth, at least 8 hours or preferably overnight. Use a slotted metal spoon or spatula to remove all the fat from the broth. Transfer the broth into two or three smaller containers. Refrigerate for up to five days or freeze for up to three months.

MAKES ABOUT 3 QUARTS ▼ SERVING SIZE 1 CUP

Nutritional information

16 calories ▼ 0.7 grams of fat

▼ ▼

1 large onion, cut into eighths

1 large leek, white part only, cut in half lengthwise, rinsed well between the layers, and cut into 2-inch pieces

4 ribs celery, trimmed and cut into 2-inch pieces

2 medium-size carrots, cut into 2-inch pieces

1 medium-size parsnip, cut into 2-inch pieces

¼ pound fresh fennel (about half a small bulb), tall stalks and leaves discarded, bulb cut into 2-inch pieces

1 pound fresh plum tomatoes, cut into quarters

2 tablespoons olive oil

Salt to taste

1 small bunch fresh parsley, rinsed

4 quarts cold water

This vegetable broth has a hearty taste that comes from roasting the vegetables. You can prepare this broth without roasting the vegetables, but the flavor is milder.

▼   ▼   ▼

Preheat the oven to 450 degrees.

Place the vegetables in a large roasting pan. Pour the olive oil over them, add the salt, and use a spatula to toss well to combine. Place the pan on the top shelf in the oven and roast until the vegetables are just beginning to turn brown, about 30 minutes.

Transfer the roasted vegetables to an 8-quart stockpot. Add the parsley and water and place over high heat. When the water boils, reduce the heat to medium-low, cover the pot, and simmer for 1 hour. Allow to stand and cool to room temperature.

Strain the broth through a large sieve or colander into a bowl or plastic container. Use a wooden spoon to press the vegetables against the sieve to extract as much of the broth as possible. Place the container in the refrigerator until thoroughly chilled and the fat has hardened on the surface of the broth, at least 8 hours or preferably overnight. Use a slotted metal spoon or spatula to remove all the fat. Divide the broth into two or three smaller containers and refrigerate or freeze. Refrigerate for up to five days days or freeze for up to three months.

MAKES ABOUT 3 QUARTS ▾ SERVING SIZE 1 CUP
Nutritional information
17 calories ▾ 1.3 grams of fat

LOW-FAT FISH BROTH

▼ ▼

2 to 3 fish frames (about 3 pounds) from white-fleshed fish

1 large leek, white part only, cut in half lengthwise, rinsed well between the layers and thickly sliced

1 large onion, cut into eighths

3 medium-size carrots, cut into 1-inch pieces

3 ribs celery, trimmed and cut into 1-inch pieces

1 bay leaf

1 heaping teaspoon dried thyme

Salt to taste

1 teaspoon black peppercorns

½ cup dry white wine

4 quarts cold water

*T*he best fish broth is made with the frames (heads with the bones and tails attached) of white-fleshed fish such as cod, pollack, sea bass, snapper, flounder, and sole. You can buy frames from your fish store. I recommend defatting the broth to ensure it's as low in fat as possible.

▼   ▼   ▼

Rinse the fish frames under cold running water to remove any gills or entrails that may remain and place them in a large 8-quart stockpot. Add the vegetables, bay leaf, thyme, salt, and peppercorns. Pour in the wine and water and place over high heat.

When the liquid boils, reduce the heat to medium-low, partially cover the pot, and cook, skimming the surface of the broth occasionally, for 30 minutes. Allow to cool to room temperature.

Remove and discard the biggest pieces of bone from the stockpot. Strain the broth into a large bowl or plastic container through a large, fine-mesh sieve. Use a wooden spoon to press the bones and vegetables against the sieve to extract as much broth as possible. Cover the container and chill thoroughly, at least 8 hours. Use a slotted metal spoon or spatula to remove any fat on the surface. Transfer the broth to smaller containers and refrigerate for up to five days or freeze for up to three months. Discard any sediment on the bottom of the container.

MAKES ABOUT 3 QUARTS ▾ SERVING SIZE 1 CUP
Nutritional information
14 calories ▾ .70 grams of fat

In addition to a flavorful, homemade broth, you should always use the best quality ingredients. Soups that are low in fat and calories need to be high in flavor, and fresh, quality ingredients will help ensure that your soups have the most delicious taste possible. Here are some tips on selecting ingredients:

- Always buy fresh produce that looks its best and avoid blemished, bruised, dried-out, or rotting fruits and vegetables.
- Buy local, seasonal produce whenever possible.
- Store fresh produce in plastic bags in the refrigerator to prevent drying out.
- Use "wild" varieties of mushrooms—crimini, shiitake, and portobello—to get the most flavorful fresh mushroom taste. Use dried mushrooms—porcini or shiitake—to add an intense mushroom flavor.
- Buy chicken and fish from reliable meat and fish markets rather than from chain supermarkets, unless yours has an outstanding butcher or fish section. Kosher chickens have the most flavor.
- Buy fish on the day you intend to cook it.
- Store potatoes and onions loose in a cool, dark place.
- Some frozen produce can be better than fresh, particularly baby peas and corn out of season. Since the sugars in these vegetables turn to starch as soon as they are harvested, fresh frozen peas and corn will likely be sweeter tasting than anything other than farm-fresh varieties. For the recipes in this book, when substituting frozen produce for fresh, always use it defrosted but not cooked.
- The best and most flavorful dried beans and grains are usually sold loose, by the pound, in health food stores and natural food supermarkets.

- My preference is to use Italian flat leaf parsley whenever parsley is called for; it's easier to chop and I prefer its taste. You can also use curly parsley.
- When using dried herbs, unless specified, avoid powdered varieties of the herb and use the dried leaves. They have a better flavor and aren't adulterated.
- Italian pasta, made from hard semolina wheat, tastes better than American-made enriched pasta, which is often produced from softer varieties of wheat.
- Canned tomatoes can vary from brand to brand. Choose tomatoes whose taste you like. My own preference is the Pomi brand (sold in boxes) or the canned, organic Muir Glen brand.
- Milk is a tricky ingredient to use in low-fat soups. It would be nice if you could simply substitute skim milk for heavy cream in recipes. The problem is that skim milk and buttermilk (which is also a nonfat milk) are unstable and curdle easily when heated. They can be added to soups, but the soups should not boil after the milk has been added.
- I have tried to select a fat/oil—even when it's a modest teaspoon—for each recipe that will enhance the flavor of the soup. Feel free to substitute fats other than those specified in any of the recipes for taste or health reasons, but please keep the quantities the same. Use a good quality oil, and avoid any oil stored in your cupboard for six months or longer, unless it hasn't been opened. You're better off investing in fresh oil. Buy a small container if you're concerned about using it on a regular basis. If you plan to use olive oil, you can use "pure" olive oil, and not "extra virgin." You can substitute oil sprays for pourable oil, which will further reduce the fat content (although the reduction is immeasurable) of the soups.

SENSATIONAL SEASONINGS

Low-fat food preparations require pungent, lively flavorings to compensate for the lack of fat, which is a natural flavor enhancer. Strong, intense, and zesty seasonings give a big boost of flavor without adding fat or calories. You'll get the most mileage from these vibrant-tasting seasonings if you add them to a soup just before serving, since cooking tends to modify and subdue flavors, even the strongest ones. Here are some lively flavorings you'll find throughout the recipes in this book.

Fresh Herbs Chopped fresh herbs, from across a broad culinary spectrum, added to a finished soup or on individual servings as a garnish, are one of my favorite ways to get fast flavor into low-fat soups. My preference is to use fresh, uncooked herbs whenever possible. (Dried herbs are all right if you use them in the cooking process but never as a garnish.) That way you'll get the strongest taste and brightest color from the herb. Normally I use one herb at a time to get a singular and distinct flavor, but occasionally you'll find the herbs in the recipes used in combinations. Combinations make for a more complex flavor and can also moderate the flavor of an herb with a particularly strong or overpowering taste, particularly rosemary and sage, which I find work best in tandem with other herbs. My favorite herbs: Italian parsley, dill, basil, tarragon, chives, mint, cilantro, chervil, rosemary, sage, and thyme. The leaves of the herb should be picked from the stems before chopping.

Lemon/Lime Juice and Zest Citrus is a good way to put some zing into a mildly flavored vegetable, fish, or fruit soup or to add a little puckery spark to an otherwise bland taste. I like the way the zest stirred into a soup gives flecks of bright green or yellow to an otherwise mildly colored soup while the juice adds most of the flavor. I have also found that lemon and lime juice are great flavor enhancers: They can bring out the best flavors from other ingredients without overpowering them. I am not partial to cooking with orange juice or zest, except in sweet fruit soups, because orange juice can be cloyingly sweet and has the tendency to overwhelm other flavors.

Peppercorns/Hot Chile Peppers/Hot Pepper Sauce Pepper is a crucial flavoring element in many of the soup recipes. Of all the ingredients that add surefire flavor to a soup, it's pepper—

black, cayenne, fresh chiles (cooked or raw), dried (whole or flakes), or in liquid form (Tabasco sauce or a generic equivalent)—that best spices up a hot or cold soup to give it added gusto. Now that most supermarkets carry fresh hot chile peppers, they are relatively easy to come by, although you may not always have a choice of hot, hotter, or hottest. Know your peppers: Bigger is often milder, smaller is usually hotter. When in doubt, ask. Always use caution when cutting up hot peppers; rinse your knife and fingers well afterward and keep your hands away from your eyes. Hot peppers are indeed *hot*, and even the residue on your fingers from handling them can sting badly.

I always keep a bottle of Tabasco sauce—a commercial mixture of vinegar, salt, and ground-up Tabasco peppers—in my spice drawer so that I can add a dash of heat without any prior recipe planning. Also in the drawer are hot pepper flakes, actually dried seeds of hot red peppers, which are a staple of Italian cooking; these are best when added to a hot soup while it's cooking.

Parmigiano-Reggiano Cheese   A sprinkling of Italian Parmigiano-Reggiano (familiarly but improperly called "Parmesan" or "Reggiano") cheese goes a long way to give a great low-fat minestrone or *pasta e fagioli* a final touch with its slightly sharp, nutty flavor that makes it perfect and authentic. Parmigiano-Reggiano has approximately 23 calories and 2 grams of fat in each grated tablespoon. You can easily use half that, 1½ teaspoons per serving, and still get a lot of flavor. Whenever cheese is called for it is optional, and not included in the calorie and fat contents of the recipe.

Salt/Soy Sauce   Salt, when used in moderation, is a great flavor enhancer; it brings out the best in most ingredients. (I understand that for a great many people salt is prohibited in the daily diet; for that reason salt in all the recipes is listed as "to taste.") I like to use kosher salt; it has neither iodine nor additives to enhance pourability. I usually add salt with my fingers, sprinkling it on rather than measuring specific quantities. I like to salt the ingredients as they cook, then taste and salt again before serving to correct the flavor. When using soy sauce for Asian soup recipes, I use a low-sodium variety. Traditionally in Asian cooking, soy sauce is never added to a dish at the table, only in cooking. As with any ingredient, you have to become comfortable with a particular type of salt or soy sauce and know its salting capabilities to be confident when you cook that you don't over- or underdo it.

Raw Onions, Shallots, Scallions, Chives, Garlic   We all know the power of raw onions and garlic—enough to keep friends afar or even make a foe—but when used carefully, moderately, and tastefully these strong flavorings can make a simple soup sensational. Yellow onions are by far the strongest in this group—*Allium cepa*—and toughest on the taste buds. As is also true of garlic, too much onion leaves a burning sensation rather than a true flavor. So when it comes to flavoring garnishes, I mostly go with chives, shallots, and scallions for a milder oniony taste. When garlic is going to be consumed uncooked, I proceed with caution—I add enough to give the flavor but not so much that it leaves a strong aftertaste.

Fresh Gingerroot   Tangy, palate-teasing gingerroot is a playful flavoring agent because it can be either sweet or savory depending on how it's used. Popular in most regions of Asia, this root, with its paper-thin skin and fibrous, stringy flesh, has a pleasant spicy and sharp taste that is particularly good in soups prepared with sweet or starchy vegetables such as carrots, potatoes, yams, and winter squash, in addition to the multitude of Asian-inspired soups. Unlike the dried, powdered version, fresh gingerroot provides a more delicate but still distinct flavor. It is an essential ingredient in Low-Fat Asian Chicken Broth where it is cooked in the soup. For a zesty ginger flavor, a pinch of freshly grated root can be added to a soup just before serving. Fresh gingerroot skin is easily peeled with a knife or vegetable peeler.

Vegetable Juices   These are an important element in a few of the cold soups you'll find in this book. Juices made from fresh vegetables have a wonderful quality that adds depth and substance to light-tasting soups.

Croutons Croutons, toasted, flavored bread cubes, are a good addition to creamy, smooth soups, adding an interesting contrast in texture as well as flavor. Although true croutons are traditionally prepared with oil or butter, you can skip the fat and simply toast the bread cubes with herbs in a 300 degree oven until completely crisp and dry to make a fat free but still very tasty version.

THE SOUP KITCHEN

Preparing soup, thankfully, doesn't require a lot of equipment or any high-tech tools. One of the most basic and rudimentary foods there is, soup can be prepared with as little as a couple of good, heavy soup pots, some stirring implements, and a tool or two for blending and pureeing. Even measuring cups, which are helpful if you are faithfully following the recipes, can be avoided, since most soups don't rely on exact measurements.

Soup Pots I recommend a stockpot for preparing broth and a smaller pot or heavy saucepan for preparing soup. I am a faithful user of the pressure cooker for preparing my broths—you can learn about preparing broth in a pressure cooker in *Cooking Under Pressure* by Lorna Sass (William Morrow, 1991), but if you are not using a pressure cooker you will need an 8- to 10-quart stockpot for making the broth recipes in this book. I suggest stainless or enameled steel stockpots. They tend to heat evenly and hold the heat well. (I usually avoid aluminum or aluminum alloy materials for pots, since aluminum is known to react with acidic ingredients and can adversely flavor the broth.)

When it comes to preparing most soups, I use a 3- to 4-quart enameled iron pot or casserole (Le Creuset is the brand I prefer) or a similarly sized heavy stainless steel saucepan. Because most soups are covered for at least some of the cooking time, these pots should have lids that fit securely. Heavy pots and pans, constructed to heat evenly and hold the heat well, cook soups best.

Spoons and Knives   You'll need some wooden spoons for stirring soups and metal spoons or spatulas for defatting broth. A good, sharp chef's knife and a paring knife are essential. A vegetable peeler can be helpful in peeling potatoes and other winter root and tuberous vegetables.

Sauté Pans, Skillets   Low-fat cooking is made a lot easier when you use pans with a nonstick coating. That way you can use a minimum of fat in your cooking; the ingredients won't stick to the pot. (In addition, they are a breeze to clean.) Many brands today—from heavy-weight, professional quality pots and pans, both foreign and domestically manufactured, to a variety of moderately priced brands—offer pans with nonstick surfaces. You should apply the same criteria when purchasing nonstick pans that you do to other pots and pans: They should be well-constructed, heat evenly, and sit flat on the stove burner. Always use plastic or wooden implements with nonstick pans to avoid scratching the surface. You will need at least one large sauté pan or skillet with a nonstick surface.

Blending Tools   Smooth, creamy soups require a tool—a blender of some variety—to make them that way. Here is a rundown on the blending choices.

Food processors: For most of my adult life I have used a food processor for the majority of my kitchen blending tasks. But food processors are not always ideal for preparing smooth soups. They are great for pureeing the solids in a soup, but when you add the broth or cooking liquid and turn the machine on, the liquid often comes pouring out from around the lid. Food processors should be used with caution and with as little liquid as possible.

Blenders: When food processors arrived on the cooking scene, blenders became less useful and I gave mine away. I bought a new blender—a classic Waring with one on/off switch—to use in testing the recipes for this book, but I quickly found that I didn't much like it. It doesn't hold enough (which means pureeing a soup in several batches), and you don't have any control. The soup is either blended smooth or it's not blended.

Hand blender (immersion blender): For testing recipes, I purchased what soon became my favorite soup-blending tool: a "handblender" by Braun. It is an all-plastic shaft, about 18 inches long, with a small metal rotary blade at the bottom that is protected by a plastic ring so it can't hit the bottom of the pot. It is hand-held with an on button that shuts off when you let it go. It can go right into the pot to blend, or partially blend, the ingredients. It doesn't splatter, unless you turn it on when it is less than fully submerged, and it is easy to clean—just rinse it off. There are no glass or plastic containers to wash. It stores in a drawer. To me, it is, by far, the most efficient blending tool.

Food mill: I use a food mill for preparing applesauce and mashed potatoes, and while one can be used to puree soups, I don't recommend it because it eliminates skins and other solids that might contribute to the flavor and texture of the soup. It's also labor intensive, both in the using and the cleaning. A more sophisticated chef's tool, a chinois (a funnel-shaped sieve with a wooden tool for pushing the ingredients through) is similarly limiting.

Soup Bowls Preheated bowls for hot soups and chilled bowls for cold soups can make a surprising difference in the quality of the soup you serve. And the shape of the bowl is integral to the enjoyment of eating the soup. I have three types of soup bowls: two-handled soup "cups" for cold or first-course soups; deep, conventional soup "bowls" for first-course smooth, creamy vegetable puree soups or for chunky chicken, fish, or seafood soups; and flat soup "plates" for main-course soups or when I want the presentation to be more dramatic. Each bowl provides a different soup experience for the eater.

CLEARLY
ELEGANT

No soup is more refined or elegant than a clear, delicate broth, garnished with a sprinkling of fresh herbs, barely cooked vegetables, or simple seafood. The king of these soups is consommé, a French invention that renders the broth so clear it shimmers like glass in your bowl. You can use any wonderfully flavored broth, consommé, or bouillon, and other flavorful broths. They will all make spectacular, show-stopping presentations for an elegant first course.

VEGETABLE CONSOMMÉ WITH ANGELHAIR PASTA AND SPINACH CHIFFONADE

▼ ▼

5 cups defatted vegetable broth, preferably homemade (page 9)

1 tablespoon tomato paste

⅓ cup dry white wine

3 large egg whites, beaten until stiff peaks form

Salt and freshly ground black pepper

½ pound angelhair pasta

1 cup packed fresh spinach leaves, thoroughly rinsed, dried, and shredded

This recipe was inspired by the Italian classic *pasta en brodo*, pasta in broth.

▼ ▼ ▼

Combine the broth, tomato paste, and wine in a heavy 6-quart saucepan over low heat and stir until the tomato paste is dissolved. Add the egg whites and use a wire whisk to stir until the mixture comes to a rolling boil. Remove the saucepan from the stove and allow it to stand 15 minutes without moving it. Line a fine-mesh sieve with several thicknesses of cheesecloth or a damp kitchen towel and place it over a clean saucepan. Pour the broth and egg white mixture through the sieve. When you are nearly ready to serve the consommé, season it with salt and pepper to taste and place it over low heat.

Bring a large pot of water to a boil over high heat. Add a tablespoon of salt and the pasta and cook, stirring frequently, until the pasta is tender, 5 to 7 minutes after the water comes back to the boil. Strain the pasta and divide it among six preheated individual soup plates. Ladle the consommé over the angel hair and garnish with the shredded spinach.

MAKES 6 SERVINGS

Nutritional information per serving
177 calories ▾ 1.8 grams of fat

MUSHROOM CONSOMMÉ WITH VEGETABLE CONFETTI

▼ ▼

1 ounce dried mushrooms, porcini, shiitake, or other variety, plus 2 pounds fresh mushrooms, stems removed, caps thinly sliced

2 cups boiling water

2 teaspoons olive oil

1 large shallot, peeled and chopped

1 cup dry white wine

4 cups water

1 teaspoon dried tarragon leaves

Salt and freshly ground black pepper

1 tablespoon dry sherry

½ cup finely diced zucchini

½ cup peeled, finely diced carrot

½ cup seeded, finely diced yellow pepper or yellow summer squash

This intensely mushroomy broth, garnished with a colorful "confetti" of cut-up vegetables, makes an exquisite soup.

▼ ▼ ▼

Combine the dried mushrooms with the boiling water in a heat-proof glass measuring cup and allow them to stand for 30 minutes.

Meanwhile, heat the oil in a heavy 6-quart saucepan over medium-high heat. Add the shallot and cook, stirring, 1 to 2 minutes. Stir in the fresh mushrooms and cook until they begin to soften, about 5 minutes. Add the wine and continue cooking until the liquid is reduced to about ½ cup, about 15 minutes. Strain the dried mushrooms and add their soaking liquid, 4 cups water, and the tarragon. Bring the liquid to a boil, reduce the heat to medium-low, and simmer until the broth has a good mushroom flavor, about 30 minutes.

Strain the mushroom broth through a sieve and pour the liquid back into the saucepan. When you are ready to serve the broth, place the saucepan over low heat, stir in the sherry, and bring to a simmer. Season with salt and pepper to taste. Combine the diced vegetables in a small mixing bowl and toss. Place a heaping tablespoon of the diced vegetables in each serving bowl, ladle the mushroom broth over the vegetables, and serve.

MAKES 6 SERVINGS

Nutritional information per serving

95 calories ▾ 2.1 grams of fat

WATERCRESS BROTH WITH MUSHROOMS AND GINGER

▼ ▼

*4 cups defatted chicken or
vegetable broth, preferably
homemade (pages 7, 9)*

*Three ¼-inch-thick slices peeled
fresh gingerroot, plus 2
teaspoons peeled and minced*

2 teaspoons corn or canola oil

*6 cups sliced mushrooms, such
as portobello, shiitake, or
crimini*

Salt

*1 bunch fresh watercress,
rinsed, dried, and finely
minced, preferably in a food
processor*

*S*triking to look at, this is a composed soup: The mushrooms are piled neatly in the center of the bowl with the green watercress consommé around them. Some fresh ginger, sprinkled on before serving, adds zest.

▼ ▼ ▼

Combine the broth with the sliced gingerroot in a heavy 6-quart saucepan over medium-high heat and bring to a boil. Reduce the heat to low and simmer for 10 minutes. Remove the ginger slices. Turn off the heat and set aside.

Meanwhile, heat the oil over medium heat in a large skillet, preferably one with a nonstick surface. Add the sliced mushrooms, season with salt to taste, and cook, stirring, until the mushrooms are tender and their liquid has mostly evaporated, 7 to 10 minutes.

Bring the broth to a simmer over medium-high heat. Add the chopped watercress and 1 teaspoon of the minced ginger. When the broth returns to the boil, cook exactly 5 minutes.

Arrange the mushrooms in piles in the center of the individual serving bowls. Carefully ladle the soup around the mushrooms. Sprinkle some of the remaining minced ginger over each serving. Serve immediately.

MAKES 6 SERVINGS
Nutritional information per serving
42 calories ▾ 2.2 grams of fat

LEMONGRASS BROTH WITH SHRIMP, BEAN SPROUTS, AND CILANTRO

▼ ▼

1 pound raw medium-size shrimp in their shells

4 cups defatted Asian chicken broth, preferably homemade (page 8)

2 cups cold water

2 sticks fresh lemongrass, peeled and cut into 2-inch pieces

1 green serrano chile, seeded and chopped

4 fresh cilantro stems, rinsed

1 tablespoon soy sauce or salt

Juice of 1 lime (about 2 tablespoons)

2 tablespoons chopped fresh cilantro leaves

4 cups fresh bean sprouts

This exotic elegant soup is delicately flavored.

▼ ▼ ▼

Peel and devein the shrimp and cut them in half lengthwise; set aside. Place the shells in a heavy 4-quart saucepan with the broth, water, lemongrass, chile, and stems of the cilantro over medium-high heat. When the liquid boils, reduce the heat to low, partially cover the saucepan, and simmer until the flavors are combined, 15 to 20 minutes. Strain and return the broth to the saucepan.

Place the saucepan over medium heat. When the broth comes to a simmer, add the shrimp and cook until pink and cooked through, about 5 minutes. Add the soy sauce or salt, lime juice, and chopped cilantro, and stir well to combine. Distribute the bean sprouts evenly among 6 individual serving bowls. Ladle the soup over the sprouts and serve immediately.

MAKES 6 SERVINGS

Nutritional information per serving
93 calories ▾ 1.2 grams of fat

UNBEATABLE BEAN SOUPS

Beans are at the heart of some of the most wonderful soups in the world. Protein rich, deliciously satisfying, and incomparably economical, bean soups are healthful, hearty, and affordably nutritious.

Although dried beans vary greatly in shape, size, and color, they all have a similar nutritional composition: 1 cup of cooked dried beans contains approximately 210 calories and 1 gram of fat, with 14 grams of protein.

While you can't deny the convenience of canned beans, my own preference is for home-cooked beans; they taste better and cost less than store-bought in a can. With a little advance preparation, you can easily cook your own: Soak beans in water at room temperature for 8 hours; drain and discard the soaking water; cook the beans in ample water until done. Most beans require 1 to 2 hours of cooking.

A pressure cooker makes cooking beans fast and doesn't require any advance preparation.

Presoak beans in a pressure cooker by cooking for 5 minutes; drain the beans; cook in ample water 10 to 20 minutes longer, depending on the variety. Always follow the manufacturer's directions for using a pressure cooker.

Whichever type of pot you choose, always discard the soaking or precooking liquid, as it contains indigestible sugar-based molecules from the beans, a leading cause of discomfort—a.k.a. gas—from eating beans. Acidic ingredients and salt tend to slow the cooking of beans, so I usually cook them without any flavorings and let them take on the taste of the soup ingredients.

COOKING TIMES FOR BEANS

TYPE	CONVENTIONAL POT	PRESSURE COOKER
Cannellini (white kidney)	1 to 1½ hours	13 to 15 minutes
Chickpeas	1½ to 2 hours	20 to 25 minutes
Fava beans	1½ to 2 hours	16 to 22 minutes
Great Northern beans	1 to 1½ hours	13 to 15 minutes
Lentils and split peas (unsoaked)	30 to 40 minutes	10 minutes
Navy beans	¾ to 1 hour	12 to 14 minutes
Pinto beans	1 to 1½ hours	14 minutes

Cooked beans can be stored, covered with cold water, in the refrigerator for up to 5 days. Strain and rinse before using.

If you use canned beans, drain and rinse them well before adding them to the soup. If possible, choose brands without additives or salt since these can adversely flavor your soup.

MIAMI BLACK BEAN SOUP

▼ ▼

2 teaspoons corn or canola oil

1 large onion, finely chopped

1 rib celery, trimmed and finely chopped

1 medium-size green bell pepper, seeded and chopped

4 medium-size cloves garlic, peeled and pressed or finely minced

¼ teaspoon red pepper flakes or 1 jalapeño pepper, seeded and chopped

1 bay leaf

4 cups cooked or canned (drained and rinsed) black beans

4 cups defatted chicken or vegetable broth, preferably homemade (pages 7, 9)

2 cups cold water

Salt and freshly ground black pepper

6 tablespoons nonfat sour cream (optional)

There's almost no restaurant in Miami that doesn't offer some version of traditional Cuban black bean soup. This recipe has a strong flavor of peppers—sweet and hot—and lots of garlic. Black beans are among the hardest of any dried bean and therefore require the longest cooking time. You can use canned beans. In Miami, black bean soup is almost always served with a dollop of sour cream. I've listed nonfat sour cream as an optional ingredient. It won't add grams of fat, only 10 calories per tablespoon.

▼ ▼ ▼

Heat the oil in a heavy 6-quart saucepan over medium-high heat. Add the onion, celery, bell pepper, and garlic and cook, stirring, until the vegetables begin to soften, 3 to 5 minutes. Add the red pepper flakes, jalapeño pepper, bay leaf, and black beans and stir well to combine with the vegetables. Stir in the broth and water and season with salt and pepper to taste. Raise the heat to high and bring to a boil. Reduce the heat to medium-low, partially cover the saucepan, and simmer until the soup is thick, about 30 minutes.

Transfer the soup in batches to a food processor or blender or use an immersion blender, and puree until the soup is smooth and turns a mauve-gray color. Return the soup to the saucepan and reheat before serving. Ladle into preheated bowls. If desired, top each serving with a tablespoon of nonfat sour cream.

MAKES 6 SERVINGS

Nutritional information per serving, without sour cream
196 calories ▾ 2.7 grams of fat

RED BEAN AND BARLEY SOUP

▼ ▼

½ cup pearl barley

2 teaspoons olive oil

1 medium-size onion, chopped

4 cups cooked or canned
(drained and rinsed) red
kidney beans

4 cups defatted chicken or
vegetable broth, preferably
homemade (pages 7, 9)

Salt

½ cup chopped fresh parsley
leaves

An incredibly robust, satisfying soup that was inspired by soups I have enjoyed in Italy. To serve this soup the way they do in Italy: Drizzle a teaspoon of extra virgin olive oil over each serving—it adds about 3.5 grams of fat and 30 calories.

▼ ▼ ▼

In a small saucepan, combine the barley with water to cover and place over medium-high heat. When the water boils, reduce the heat to low and simmer for 5 minutes. Drain the barley, rinse, and drain again. Set aside.

Heat the oil in a heavy 4-quart saucepan over medium-high heat. Add the onion and cook, stirring, until it begins to soften, 2 to 3 minutes. Stir in the beans and broth and bring to a boil. Reduce heat to medium-low, cover the saucepan, and cook 15 minutes.

Use a slotted spoon to transfer the beans and onions to a food processor and turn the machine on and off 4 or 5 times to finely chop the beans but not puree them. Scrape the sides of the work-bowl down and pulse the machine on and off once or twice more. Return the beans to the saucepan with the liquid and stir well to blend. Add the barley and place over medium-high heat. When the soup comes to a boil, reduce the heat to low and simmer, stirring frequently to prevent the barley from sticking, until the barley is tender, about 30 minutes. Stir in the parsley, season with salt to taste, and serve.

MAKES 6 SERVINGS
Nutritional information per serving
243 calories ▼ 2.8 grams of fat

▼ ▼

2 teaspoons olive oil

1 medium-size onion, finely
   chopped

2 large cloves garlic, peeled and
   pressed or finely minced

4 cups cooked or canned
   (drained and rinsed)
   cannellini beans or other
   white beans such as Great
   Northern or navy

2 cups canned chopped
   tomatoes, with their juices

1 fresh sage leaf

4 cups defatted chicken or
   vegetable broth, preferably
   homemade (pages 7, 9)

Salt and freshly ground black
   pepper

¼ cup chopped fresh parsley
   leaves

A rich, robust soup, inspired by traditional recipes for Tuscan beans, that makes a perfect light lunch main course when served with a salad and some good crusty bread.

▼ ▼ ▼

Heat the oil in a heavy 4-quart saucepan over medium-high heat. Add the onion and garlic and cook, stirring, until the onion begins to soften, 2 to 3 minutes. Stir in the beans, tomatoes, and sage leaf. Add the broth. Turn the heat to high and bring to a boil. Reduce the heat to low, cover the saucepan, and simmer for 20 minutes. Remove and discard the sage leaf.

Transfer the soup to a food processor or blender and puree or use an immersion blender. Return the soup to the saucepan. Season with salt and pepper to taste. Reheat before serving if necessary. Stir in the parsley just before serving.

MAKES 6 SERVINGS
Nutritional information per serving
218 calories ▾ 2.6 grams of fat

WHITE BEAN AND RADICCHIO SOUP

▼ ▼

2 teaspoons olive oil

1 medium-size onion, finely chopped

2 large cloves garlic, peeled and pressed or finely minced

4 cups cooked or canned (drained and rinsed) cannellini beans

4 cups defatted chicken or vegetable broth, preferably homemade (pages 7, 9)

2 cups finely shredded radicchio (about ¼ pound)

Salt

2 tablespoons chopped fresh parsley leaves

*G*arlic and cannellini beans give this soup a creamy heartiness. The radicchio adds subtle color and a slightly bitter flavor that offsets the richness of the beans. I like to puree half the soup and leave the rest chunky. If you don't have radicchio, use a bitter green, such as escarole.

▼ ▼ ▼

Heat the oil in a heavy 4-quart saucepan over medium-high heat. Add the onion and garlic and cook, stirring, until the onion begins to soften, 2 to 3 minutes. Stir in the beans and broth and bring to a boil. Reduce the heat to medium-low, cover the saucepan, and simmer for 20 minutes.

Transfer about half the soup to a food processor or blender and process until smooth. Pour the pureed soup back into the saucepan and stir well to combine with the unpureed soup. Place over medium-high heat and bring the soup back to a simmer. Stir in the radicchio and cook until it is wilted and tender, about 5 minutes. Season with salt to taste. Garnish each serving with a pinch of the parsley.

MAKES 6 SERVINGS

Nutritional information per serving

204 calories ▾ 2.5 grams of fat

GARLICKY WHITE BEAN AND SPINACH SOUP

▼ ▼

2 teaspoons olive oil

1 medium-size onion, finely chopped

2 large cloves garlic, peeled and pressed or finely minced

2 cups cooked or canned (drained and rinsed) small white beans such as navy or Great Northern beans

4 cups defatted chicken or vegetable broth, preferably homemade (pages 7, 9)

Salt

10-ounce package fresh spinach, tough stems removed, thoroughly rinsed, and coarsely chopped

Freshly ground black pepper

*L*ots of garlic and the creamy puree of white beans help make this a thick and rich-tasting soup.

▼ ▼ ▼

Heat the oil in a heavy 4-quart saucepan over medium-high heat. Add the onion and garlic and cook, stirring, until the onion begins to soften, 2 to 3 minutes. Add the beans and broth. Season with salt to taste. Raise the heat to high and bring to a boil. Reduce the heat to medium-low, partially cover the saucepan, and simmer until the soup has thickened slightly, about 15 minutes. Add the spinach and cook 5 minutes until wilted, about 5 minutes longer. Transfer the soup in batches to a food processor or blender and puree or use an immersion blender. Return the soup to the saucepan; add salt and pepper to taste. Reheat over medium-low heat and serve.

MAKES 6 SERVINGS
Nutritional information per serving
152.3 calories ▼ 3.3 grams of fat

SOUP OF CHICKPEAS, PASTA, AND ROSEMARY

▼ ▼

1 teaspoon olive oil

1 medium-size onion, finely chopped

1 medium-size clove garlic, peeled and pressed or finely minced

2 cups cooked or canned (drained and rinsed) chickpeas

1 tablespoon fresh rosemary leaves, coarsely chopped

4 cups defatted chicken or vegetable broth, preferably homemade (pages 7, 9)

Pinch of red pepper flakes

½ cup short tube-shaped pasta, such as ditalini or tubetti

Salt

*G*reat, strong flavors make this a superb soup. Use only fresh rosemary and preferably a short tube-shaped macaroni.

▼ ▼ ▼

Heat the oil in a heavy 4-quart saucepan over medium-high heat. Add the onion and garlic and cook, stirring, until the onion begins to soften, 2 to 3 minutes; be careful not to burn the garlic. Add the chickpeas, rosemary, broth, and pepper flakes and bring to a boil. Cover, reduce the heat to medium, and simmer for 10 minutes. Stir in the pasta, raise the heat to medium-high, and cook, stirring frequently to prevent sticking, until the pasta is tender but firm (al dente), about 10 minutes longer. Season with salt to taste.

MAKES 6 SERVINGS
Nutritional information per serving
149 calories ▾ 2.9 grams of fat

LEMONY CHICKPEA AND ESCAROLE SOUP

▼ ▼

1 teaspoon olive oil

1 large onion, finely chopped

*2 medium-size cloves garlic,
peeled and pressed or finely
minced*

*2 cups cooked or canned
(drained and rinsed)
chickpeas*

*4 cups defatted chicken or
vegetable broth, preferably
homemade (pages 7, 9)*

*1 small head escarole, roughly
chopped to yield about 6 cups*

1 tablespoon fresh lemon juice

*Salt and freshly ground black
pepper*

*2 tablespoons chopped fresh
parsley leaves*

A blend of chickpeas and broth is the rich-tasting base of this robust and savory soup. The sharp bitterness of the escarole balances the almost sweet flavor of the beans. If you prepare this soup ahead of time, the escarole will turn from a fresh, bright green color to a darker hue as it cooks or stands; this doesn't affect the flavor.

▼ ▼ ▼

Heat the oil in a heavy 4-quart saucepan over medium-high heat. Add the onion and garlic and cook, stirring, until the onion begins to soften, 2 to 3 minutes. Add the chickpeas and broth and bring to a boil. Reduce the heat to medium-low, cover the saucepan, and simmer until the onion is completely tender and the flavors are combined, 15 to 20 minutes.

Transfer the soup to a food processor or blender or use an immersion blender, and pulse the machine on and off a few times. The chickpeas should be broken up and coarsely chopped, not smooth. You can prepare the soup ahead of time to this point.

Return the soup to the saucepan and place over medium heat. Add the escarole and continue cooking, stirring occasionally, until it is tender, 7 to 10 minutes longer. Stir in the lemon juice and season with salt and pepper to taste. Ladle into bowls and garnish with parsley.

MAKES 6 SERVINGS
Nutritional information per serving
129 calories ▾ 2.8 grams of fat

PASTA E FAGIOLI

▼ ▼

1 medium-size onion, cut into
    8 pieces

2 medium-size carrots, cut into
    2-inch pieces

1 rib celery, trimmed and cut
    into 1-inch pieces

¼ pound fresh fennel (about
    half a small bulb), tall stalks
    and leaves discarded and bulb
    cut into cubes

1 large clove garlic, peeled

2 teaspoons olive oil

2 cups canned chopped
    tomatoes, with their juices

4 cups defatted chicken or
    vegetable broth, preferably
    homemade (pages 7, 9)

1 cup cooked or canned
    (drained and rinsed) white
    beans, such as Great
    Northern, navy, or cannellini

½ cup short tube-shaped pasta,
    such as ditalini or tubetti

Salt and freshly ground black
    pepper

2 tablespoons chopped fresh
    basil leaves

2 tablespoons chopped fresh
    parsley leaves

2 tablespoons freshly grated
    Parmigiano-Reggiano cheese
    (optional)

*P*asta e fagioli can be any soup of pasta and beans; as with mine-strone, every region of Italy has its own variation. This version is a favorite in my house. I sometimes change the pasta type or use smaller or larger white beans. It's always a crowd pleaser.

▼ ▼ ▼

Combine the onion, carrots, celery, fennel, and garlic in a food processor and process until the vegetables are finely chopped, about 15 seconds (or finely chop by hand).

Heat the oil in a heavy 4-quart saucepan over medium-high heat. Add the chopped vegetables and cook, stirring, until they begin to soften, 2 to 3 minutes. Stir in the tomatoes and broth and bring to a boil. Cover, reduce the heat to medium-low, and sim-mer for 20 to 30 minutes. Add the beans and pasta and cook, stir-ring frequently, until the pasta is tender but firm (al dente), about 10 minutes. Season with salt and pepper to taste. Stir in the basil and parsley. Garnish each serving with some of the cheese, if desired.

MAKES 6 SERVINGS
Nutritional information per serving without the cheese
138 calories ▾ 2.5 grams of fat

▼ ▼

2 teaspoons corn, canola, or
  olive oil

1 medium-size onion, finely
  chopped

2 medium-size carrots, cut in
  half lengthwise, and sliced
  ½ inch thick

1 rib celery, trimmed and finely
  chopped

2 cups dried split peas, picked
  over and rinsed

4 cups defatted chicken or
  vegetable broth, preferably
  homemade (pages 7, 9)

2 cups cold water

Salt and freshly ground black
  pepper

I could never figure out how split pea soup got a bad rap with kids. I've always loved this soup and have found it to be a great base for all kinds of ingredients. You can add pasta or rice to it, all manner of fresh herbs (dill is particularly good), and of course meat and ham bones to make it richer. I usually make this soup in my pressure cooker because it requires only 10 minutes of cooking time. Here's the basic stovetop recipe.

▼ ▼ ▼

Heat the oil in a heavy 4-quart saucepan over medium-high heat. Add the onion, carrots, and celery and cook, stirring, until the vegetables begin to soften, 2 to 3 minutes. Add the split peas, broth, and water and bring to a boil. Partially cover the saucepan, reduce the heat to medium-low, and simmer until the soup is thick, about 45 minutes. Season with salt and pepper to taste before serving.

MAKES 6 SERVINGS

Nutritional information per serving
233 calories ▾ 2.7 grams of fat

LUSCIOUS LENTIL SOUP

▼ ▼

2 teaspoons olive oil

1 medium-size onion, finely chopped

1 medium-size carrot, finely chopped

1 rib celery, trimmed and finely chopped

2 cups dried brown lentils, picked over and rinsed

4 cups defatted chicken or vegetable broth, preferably homemade (pages 7, 9)

2 cups cold water

Salt and freshly ground black pepper

I've been preparing this soup for as long as I've been able to cook, and it's always gratifying. I usually prepare it in a pressure cooker; it only requires 10 minutes of cooking time. Use smaller brown lentils if they're available; I find they have the best flavor and hold their shape better than larger lentils.

▼ ▼ ▼

Heat the oil in a heavy 4-quart saucepan over medium-high heat. Add the onion, carrot, and celery and cook, stirring, until the vegetables begin to soften, 2 to 3 minutes. Add the lentils, broth and water and bring to a boil. Partially cover the saucepan, reduce the heat to medium-low, and simmer until the lentils are soft and the soup is thick, about 45 minutes.

Transfer about half the soup to a food processor or blender or use an immersion blender, and pulse the machine a few times to lightly blend the soup. Return the soup to the saucepan, stir to combine with the unpureed soup, season with salt and pepper, and heat through before serving.

MAKES 6 SERVINGS
Nutritional information per serving
231 calories ▾ 2.7 grams of fat

LENTIL AND PORTOBELLO MUSHROOM SOUP

▾ ▾

2 teaspoons olive oil

1 medium-size onion, finely chopped

1 pound portobello mushrooms (or substitute other mushrooms, preferably crimini or shiitake), stems removed, caps coarsely chopped

1 cup canned chopped tomatoes, with their juices

1 cup dried brown lentils, picked over and rinsed

5 cups defatted chicken or vegetable broth, preferably homemade (pages 7, 9)

Salt

½ cup chopped fresh parsley leaves

*E*arthy rustic flavors make this wholesome soup satisfying enough to serve as a main course.

▾ ▾ ▾

Heat the oil in a heavy 4-quart saucepan over medium-high heat. Add the onion and cook, stirring, until it begins to soften, 2 to 3 minutes. Add the mushrooms and continue cooking, stirring occasionally, until they soften and begin to release their liquid, about 5 minutes. Stir in the tomatoes, lentils, and broth and bring to a boil. Reduce the heat to low, cover the saucepan, and simmer until the soup has thickened and the lentils are tender, about 1 hour. Season with salt to taste, stir in the parsley, and serve.

MAKES 6 SERVINGS
Nutritional information per serving
147 calories ▾ 2.6 grams of fat

THREE-BEAN MINESTRA WITH SWISS CHARD

▼ ▼

1 teaspoon olive oil

1 medium-size red onion, finely chopped

2 medium-size carrots, finely chopped

Pinch of red pepper flakes, or more to taste

4 cups defatted chicken or vegetable broth, preferably homemade (pages 7, 9)

2 cups cold water

2 tablespoons tomato paste

1 cup cooked or canned (drained and rinsed) chickpeas

1 cup cooked or canned (drained and rinsed) red kidney beans

1 cup cooked or canned (drained and rinsed) white beans, such as cannellini, Great Northern, or navy

1 bunch Swiss chard, stems removed, thoroughly rinsed, and leaves finely chopped

½ cup chopped fresh parsley leaves

Salt and freshly ground black pepper

This is a very tasty, colorful soup with bold flavors . You can substitute fresh spinach for the chard.

▼ ▼ ▼

Heat the oil in a heavy 4-quart saucepan over medium-high heat. Add the onion, carrots, and pepper flakes and cook, stirring, until the vegetables begin to soften, 2 to 3 minutes. Stir in the broth, water, and tomato paste and stir until the tomato paste is dissolved. Add the chickpeas, kidney beans, and white beans and bring to a boil. Partially cover the saucepan, reduce the heat to medium-low, and simmer for about 20 minutes. Add the Swiss chard, stir, and continue cooking until it is tender, 5 to 7 minutes longer. Season with salt and pepper to taste, and serve.

MAKES 6 SERVINGS
Nutritional information per serving
177 calories ▾ 2.4 grams of fat

FAVA BEAN AND SWISS CHARD SOUP

▼ ▼

2 teaspoons olive oil

1 medium-size onion, finely chopped

1 large clove garlic, peeled and pressed or finely minced

4 cups cooked or canned (drained and rinsed) dried fava beans

4 cups defatted chicken or vegetable broth, preferably homemade (pages 7, 9)

2 cups cold water

1 bunch Swiss chard, stems removed, thoroughly rinsed, and leaves roughly chopped

Salt and freshly ground black pepper

*T*his is a hearty, chunky soup with the outgoing, forthright flavor of fava beans. Use only dried and cooked favas or canned favas; fresh uncooked favas from their pods won't give the right taste or texture. Use a food processor to get the coarse consistency of the finished soup.

▼ ▼ ▼

Heat the oil in a heavy 4-quart saucepan over medium-high heat. Add the onion and garlic and cook, stirring, until the onion begins to soften, 2 to 3 minutes. Add the favas, broth, and water and bring to a boil. Partially cover the saucepan, reduce the heat to medium-low, and simmer for 15 minutes. Stir in the Swiss chard until it is incorporated into the soup. Continue cooking, uncovered, until the chard is tender and has turned a dark-green color, about 5 minutes.

Transfer the soup to a food processor. Pulse the machine on and off three or four times to blend the favas and chard but don't puree the soup. The texture should be quite thick and chunky. Return the soup to the saucepan and reheat before serving. Season with salt and pepper to taste.

MAKES 6 SERVINGS

Nutritional information per serving
120 calories ▾ 2.7 grams of fat

FROM THE SEA

An abundance of magnificent fresh fish and exquisite shellfish characterizes these sturdy soup recipes. With outstanding flavor, each serving is satisfying enough to be the centerpiece of a meal when served with a salad and some good bread.

All of these soups are best when served as soon as they are prepared. Fish and shellfish should be cooked just until done—after that, fish falls apart and shellfish tends to toughen when they're overcooked or reheated—so care should be taken in the preparation. Always buy your fish and shellfish from reliable fishmongers on the day you intend to cook it.

MEDITERRANEAN FISH SOUP

▼ ▼

1½ pounds white-fleshed fish
   fillets such as cod, pollack, or
   monkfish, cut into 2-inch pieces

3 large cloves garlic, pressed or
   finely minced

½ teaspoon saffron threads
   steeped in ½ cup boiling water

2 teaspoons olive oil

1 medium-size onion, finely
   chopped

1 large leek, white part only,
   cut in half lengthwise, rinsed
   well between the layers, and
   thinly sliced

1 rib celery, trimmed and thinly
   sliced

¼ pound fresh fennel (about
   half a small bulb), tall stalks
   and leaves discarded and bulb
   thinly sliced

2 cups canned chopped
   tomatoes, with their juices

½ teaspoon fennel seeds

3 cups defatted fish broth,
   preferably homemade
   (page 10)

1 tablespoon tomato paste

Salt and freshly ground black
   pepper

2 tablespoons chopped fresh
   parsley leaves

*I*nspired by many Mediterranean-style fish soups I've enjoyed—
bouillabaisse and *bourride* in France, *cacciucco* and *zuppa di pesce* in
Italy—this tomato-based soup has traditional southern European
flavorings including fresh fennel, leeks, lots of saffron, garlic, and
well-seasoned fish broth. You can use a mixture of fish and shellfish, but keep the quantities the same and use only the freshest fish.

▼ ▼ ▼

Combine the fish, garlic, and half the saffron-and-water mixture
in a small mixing bowl. Toss well and allow to stand at room temperature while you prepare the soup.

Heat the oil in a heavy 4-quart saucepan over medium-high heat.
Add the onion and leek and cook, stirring, until the onion begins
to soften, 2 to 3 minutes. Add the celery and fennel bulb and
continue to cook, stirring, until the celery has softened slightly,
about 3 minutes longer. Add the chopped tomatoes, fennel seeds,
and fish broth and bring to a boil. Reduce the heat to low, cover
the casserole, and simmer until the vegetables are tender, about
20 minutes. Uncover the pot and stir in the remaining saffron-
and-water mixture and the tomato paste. Season with salt and
pepper to taste. Continue cooking for 5 minutes longer. Add the
fish and cook, stirring occasionally, until the fish flakes easily
with a fork, about 10 minutes. Garnish each serving with some of
the parsley and serve.

MAKES 6 SERVINGS
Nutritional information per serving
165 calories ▾ 3.0 grams of fat

FRENCH FISH CHOWDER

▾ ▾

2 teaspoons olive oil

2 medium-size onions, finely chopped

1 medium-size Idaho potato, peeled and cut into medium-size dice

1 large bouquet garni containing 1 small bunch fresh parsley, 5 cloves peeled garlic, 1 teaspoon whole cloves, ½ teaspoon black peppercorns, 3 sprigs fresh thyme or pinch dried thyme, all wrapped securely in several thicknesses of cheesecloth and secured with kitchen string

1½ pounds white-fleshed fish fillets, preferably cod or pollack, cut into 2-inch pieces

2 cups dry white wine

4 cups water or defatted fish broth, preferably homemade (page 10)

Salt and freshly ground black pepper

½ teaspoon cayenne pepper

2 tablespoons chopped fresh parsley leaves

*T*his is a traditional recipe from the Atlantic coast of France. The great flavor of this chowder depends on the bouquet garni, plus white wine and lots of fresh garlic. Water, not broth, is used to prepare this soup but you can use fish broth if you want a more intense flavor. Use only the freshest white-fleshed ocean fish, preferably cod or pollack.

▾ ▾ ▾

Heat the oil in a heavy 4-quart saucepan over medium-high heat. Add the onions and cook, stirring, until softened, 2 to 3 minutes. Add the potato, bouquet garni, fish, wine, and water or broth. Increase the heat to high and bring to a boil. Partially cover the saucepan, reduce the heat to medium-low, and simmer until the potato is tender and the fish flakes easily with a fork, about 15 minutes.

Remove the bouquet garni from the pot. Pour the fish chowder through a sieve. Transfer the fish-and-potato mixture to a bowl to keep warm and return the liquid to the saucepan over medium heat. Simmer to reduce the liquid and concentrate the flavor, 20 to 25 minutes longer. Season with salt and pepper to taste and stir in the cayenne pepper.

To serve, divide the fish-and-potato mixture evenly among six soup bowls and pour the soup over the fish. Garnish with the parsley and serve.

MAKES 6 SERVINGS

Nutritional information per serving
209 calories ▾ 2.9 grams of fat

MUSSEL AND WHITE BEAN SOUP

▼ ▼

2 large shallots, finely chopped to yield ½ cup

4 large cloves garlic, pressed or finely minced

Pinch of red pepper flakes

4 pounds fresh mussels, shells scrubbed and debearded (discard any with broken or open shells that won't shut)

2 cups dry white wine

1 cup cold water

1 teaspoon olive oil

1 pound (about 6) fresh plum tomatoes, peeled, seeded, and diced

1 cup cooked or canned (drained and rinsed) white beans, such as Great Northern, cannellini, or navy

2 tablespoons chopped fresh parsley leaves

Salt and freshly ground black pepper

*P*lace the shallots, 2 cloves of the garlic, and the red pepper flakes in a heavy 8-quart pot. Add the mussels. Pour in the wine and water. Cover the pot, place over high heat, and cook until the mussel shells are open, about 5 minutes. Pour the mussels and their cooking liquid through a sieve lined with several thicknesses of cheesecloth. Reserve the cooking liquid and place it in a small saucepan. You should have about 4 cups. Place the saucepan with the cooking liquid over medium-high heat. Simmer until the liquid has been reduced to 3 cups, about 15 minutes. Turn off the heat and set aside.

Take 18 of the mussels in their shells, place in a small bowl, and cover with aluminum foil to keep warm. Remove the remaining mussels from their shells, discarding any that haven't opened, and set aside. In a separate heavy 4- or 6-quart saucepan, heat the oil over medium-high heat. Add the remaining 2 cloves of garlic and the tomatoes and cook, stirring, until the tomatoes turn pink and lose their raw red color, 2 to 3 minutes. Add the white beans and shelled mussels, stir in the reduced cooking liquid and simmer until the soup is hot, about 5 minutes. Add the parsley and season with salt and pepper to taste. To serve, ladle the soup into individual serving bowls and garnish each serving with 3 of the reserved mussels in their shells.

MAKES 6 SERVINGS

Nutritional information per serving

189 calories ▾ 2.9 grams of fat

MUSSEL SOUP WITH THYME

▼ ▼

3 to 4 medium-size bunches
  fresh thyme (2 ounces) or
  ¼ cup dried thyme

2 large cloves garlic, peeled and
  pressed or finely minced

1 medium-size shallot, finely
  minced

5 pounds fresh mussels,
  scrubbed and debearded
  (discard any with broken or
  open shells that will not shut)

2 cups dry white wine

1 cup cold water

I was served this soup in a Paris bistro called Le Dôme. It requires quite a lot of thyme, either fresh or dried, and the more the better.

▼ ▼ ▼

Place the thyme in the bottom of a heavy 8-quart stockpot. Add the garlic, shallot, and mussels. Pour the wine and water over the mussels, cover the pot, and place over medium-high heat. When the liquid boils, reduce the heat to medium-low, and simmer until all the mussels have opened, about 5 minutes. Discard any mussels that remain tightly closed. Spoon the mussels into individual serving bowls. Discard the sprigs of thyme, ladle the "soup" loaded with thyme leaves from the bottom of the pot over the mussels, and serve.

MAKES 6 SERVINGS

Nutritional information per serving
164 calories ▼ 2.9 grams of fat

PUREE OF LEEK AND CELERY ROOT WITH FRESH CRABMEAT AND DILL

▼ ▼

2 teaspoons olive oil

1 large leek, white part only,
cut in half lengthwise, rinsed
well between the layers, and
sliced ½ inch thick

1 large celery root (about
1 pound), peeled and cut
into 1-inch pieces

5 cups defatted chicken or
vegetable broth, preferably
homemade (pages 7, 9)

Salt

½ pound cooked crabmeat,
well drained (defrosted if
frozen)

2 tablespoons chopped fresh dill
leaves

*C*reamy and delicately infused with the flavor of celery, this is a luxurious and delicious soup. Cooked crabmeat is stirred in at the very end as an elegant garnish.

▼ ▼ ▼

Heat the oil in a heavy 4-quart saucepan over medium-high heat. Add the leek and cook, stirring, until it begins to soften, 2 to 3 minutes. Stir in the celery root and broth and bring to a boil. Reduce the heat to medium-low, cover the saucepan, and simmer until the celery root is completely tender when pierced with a sharp knife, about 30 minutes.

Transfer the soup to a food processor or blender or use an immersion blender, and process until smooth. Return the soup to the saucepan and season with salt to taste. Just before serving, place the saucepan over medium-low heat and bring to a simmer. Add the crabmeat and cook until it is heated through, about 5 minutes. Stir in the dill and serve.

MAKES 6 SERVINGS

Nutritional information per serving
106 calories ▼ 2.8 grams of fat

LEEK, TOMATO, AND SHRIMP CHOWDER

▼ ▼

2 teaspoons olive oil

2 large leeks, white part only, cut in half lengthwise, rinsed well between the layers, and thinly sliced

2 medium-size yellow boiling potatoes, such as Yukon Gold or Yellow Finn, peeled, cut into quarters, and thinly sliced

2 cups canned chopped tomatoes, with their juices

2 tablespoons tomato paste

4 cups defatted chicken or vegetable broth, preferably homemade (pages 7, 9)

1 pound raw small shrimp, peeled, deveined, and cut into ½-inch pieces

2 tablespoons chopped fresh chives

*S*avory but subtle, the leek, tomato, and shrimp form a compelling complement of flavors in this exquisite chowder.

▼ ▼ ▼

Heat the oil in a heavy 4-quart saucepan over medium-high heat. Add the leeks and cook, stirring, until they begin to soften, 2 to 3 minutes. Add the potatoes, tomatoes, tomato paste, and broth and bring the liquid to a boil. Reduce the heat to medium-low, cover the saucepan and simmer until the potatoes are tender when pierced with a sharp knife, about 20 minutes. Stir in the shrimp and cook until they are pink and cooked through, about 5 minutes longer. Garnish each serving with the chives and serve.

MAKES 6 SERVINGS
Nutritional information per serving
145 calories ▾ 2.9 grams of fat

CREAMY FENNEL SOUP WITH SHRIMP

▼ ▼

1 pound fresh fennel (about 1 large bulb), tall stalks and leaves discarded and bulb cut into 2-inch pieces

1 medium-size onion, finely chopped

1 medium-size yellow boiling potato, such as Yellow Finn or Yukon Gold, peeled and diced

4 cups defatted chicken or vegetable broth, preferably homemade (pages 7, 9)

Salt and freshly ground black pepper

½ pound raw small shrimp, peeled and deveined

3 scallions, green part only, thinly sliced

This is a luxurious but light soup that is elegant enough to serve at your most formal dinner party. Still, it's incredibly easy to make and you can prepare it well in advance. Slivered scallion greens add just a hint of sharpness to offset the creamy flavor.

▼ ▼ ▼

Combine the fennel, onion, potato, and broth in a heavy 4-quart saucepan over medium-high heat. Bring the broth to a boil, cover the saucepan, reduce the heat to medium-low, and simmer until the fennel and potato are tender when pierced with a sharp knife, about 20 minutes.

Use a slotted spoon to transfer the vegetables from the soup to a food processor or blender and process until smooth. Return the pureed vegetables to the broth and stir well to combine. Season with salt and pepper to taste. Cover and reheat before serving.

Meanwhile, bring a small saucepan of water to a boil over high heat. Add the shrimp and when the water comes back to a boil, cook for 1 minute. Drain. Place some of the shrimp (approximately 6) in a pile in the center of the individual serving bowls. Ladle the soup around the shrimp, garnish each serving with some of the scallion greens, and serve.

MAKES 6 SERVINGS

Nutritional information per serving
86 calories ▾ 1.0 grams of fat

LEGAL SEA FOODS' LIGHT CLAM CHOWDER

▼ ▼

2 cups chopped fresh quahogs
   (sea clams) or other chopped
   clams

4 cups defatted fish broth,
   preferably homemade
   (page 10)

1 small onion, finely chopped
   (to yield ½ cup)

1 medium-size clove garlic

1 bay leaf

¼ teaspoon dried thyme leaves

3 ribs celery, trimmed and
   finely diced

1 large carrot, finely diced

1 medium-size yellow boiling
   potato, such as Yukon Gold
   or Yellow Finn, peeled and
   finely diced

Salt

1 teaspoon freshly ground black
   pepper

1 tablespoon chopped fresh
   parsley leaves

*L*egal Sea Foods Inc., a chain of restaurants and fish markets, has been an institution in Boston for thirty years, and its chowders—fish and clam—have been a staple of the business; they were even served at several presidential inaugurations. Then, in 1988, to meet the changing times, Legal introduced a light version of its clam chowder. This peppery-tasting recipe first appeared in *The New York Times* in an article I wrote about Legal Sea Foods' chowders.

▼ ▼ ▼

Combine the quahogs, fish broth, onion, garlic, bay leaf, and thyme in a heavy 4-quart saucepan over high heat. When the liquid boils, reduce the heat to medium-low, cover, and simmer for 10 minutes. Add the celery, carrot, and potato and cook about 30 minutes longer. Season with salt and pepper; stir in the parsley just before serving.

MAKES 6 SERVINGS
Nutritional information per serving
118 calories ▾ 1.6 grams of fat

NEW ENGLAND LOBSTER AND CORN CHOWDER

▼ ▼

1 teaspoon corn or canola oil

1 large onion, chopped

1 large yellow boiling potato
(about ½ pound), such as
Yukon Gold or Yellow Finn,
peeled and diced

2 cups fresh corn kernels or one
10-ounce package frozen
corn, defrosted

8 sprigs fresh thyme

4 cups defatted chicken or fish
broth, preferably homemade
(pages 7, 10)

1 cup cold water

1 cup buttermilk

1 pound cooked lobster meat,
cut into bite-size pieces (taken
from four 1-pound lobsters or
bought already cooked)

Salt and freshly ground black
pepper

2 tablespoons chopped fresh
parsley leaves

*T*he inspiration for this recipe comes from Boston chef Jasper White's recipe.

▼ ▼ ▼

Heat the oil in a heavy 4-quart saucepan over medium-high heat. Add the onion and cook, stirring, until it begins to soften, 2 to 3 minutes. Add the potato, corn, and thyme; stir in the broth and water and bring to a boil. Reduce the heat to medium-low, cover the saucepan, and simmer until the potato is tender when pierced with a sharp knife, about 20 minutes. Remove the thyme sprigs. Stir in the buttermilk and lobster meat and cook until the lobster is heated through, 5 to 7 minutes. Season with salt and pepper to taste, garnish each serving with some of the parsley, and serve.

MAKES 6 SERVINGS
Nutritional information per serving
208 calories ▾ 2.6 grams of fat

NEW YORK RED CLAM CHOWDER

▼ ▼

2 teaspoons corn or canola oil

1 medium-size onion, finely chopped

2 large yellow boiling potatoes (about 1 pound), Yellow Finn or Yukon Gold, peeled and cut into medium-size dice

2 cups canned chopped tomatoes, with their juices

1 cup dry white wine

2 cups cold water

1 teaspoon dried thyme leaves

Salt and freshly ground black pepper

2 cups chopped clams, with their juices

2 tablespoons chopped fresh parsley leaves

The difference between New York and New England clam chowder is simple. Tomatoes—and no milk—make chowder New York style.

▼ ▼ ▼

Heat the oil in a heavy 4-quart saucepan over medium-high heat. Add the onion and cook, stirring, until it begins to soften, 2 to 3 minutes. Stir in the potatoes, tomatoes, wine, water, and thyme and season with salt and pepper to taste. Bring to a boil. Reduce the heat to medium-low, partially cover the saucepan, and simmer until the potatoes are tender when pierced with a sharp knife, about 20 minutes. Add the clams and cook 10 minutes longer. Add the parsley and serve.

MAKES 6 SERVINGS

Nutritional information per serving

199 calories ▾ 2.9 grams of fat

OYSTER CHOWDER

▼ ▼

1 teaspoon unsalted butter

1 large onion, finely chopped

2 ribs celery, trimmed and chopped

1 large yellow boiling potato (about ½ pound), such as Yellow Finn or Yukon Gold, peeled and diced

2 cups defatted fish broth, preferably homemade (page 10)

2 cups shucked oysters, drained of their juices

Salt and freshly ground black pepper

1 cup buttermilk

2 tablespoons chopped fresh parsley leaves

Ground nutmeg

A creamy, luscious soup that will please any oyster lover. You can buy shucked oysters at most good fishmarkets. If they don't have them on hand, they can usually get them for you. The recipe calls for a little butter in the beginning to give the soup some extra rich flavor.

▼ ▼ ▼

Heat the butter in a heavy 4-quart saucepan over medium-high heat. Add the onion, celery, and potato and cook, stirring, until the onion begins to soften, 2 to 3 minutes. Add the broth and bring to a boil. Reduce the heat to medium-low, cover the saucepan, and simmer until the potato is tender, 15 to 20 minutes. Transfer the soup to a food processor or blender or use an immersion blender, and process until smooth. Return the soup to the saucepan and place over medium-high heat. When the soup begins to simmer, add the oysters and cook until the oysters are cooked through but still tender (overcooking will cause the oysters to become tough) and the soup is hot, about 10 minutes. Season with salt and pepper to taste. Stir in the buttermilk and cook about 1 minute longer to heat through. Serve the soup in flat soup plates, if possible. Garnish each serving with some fresh parsley and a pinch of nutmeg.

MAKES 6 SERVINGS
Nutritional information per serving
120 calories ▾ 3.0 grams of fat

GOOD AND GOOD FOR YOU: CHICKEN SOUPS

▼ ▼ ▼ ▼ ▼ ▼ ▼ ▼ ▼ ▼ ▼ ▼ ▼ ▼ ▼ ▼ ▼ ▼ ▼ ▼

There are few things in life as comforting as a bowl of chicken soup. Even though its medicinal qualities can't be scientifically measured, chicken soup sure does make you feel good. Chicken soup is the most universally loved of all soups, and these recipes reflect just how global the appeal is.

All these recipes call for a half-pound of white-meat, skinless, boneless chicken. A half-pound of chicken, even for six, is generous yet the fat and calorie content of the soups remains quite low. You can further reduce the amount of chicken to make these soups even lower in fat and calories.

HOME-STYLE CHICKEN AND VEGETABLE SOUP

▼ ▼

1 teaspoon olive oil

½ pound boneless, skinless white-meat chicken, cut into 1-inch pieces

Salt

1 medium-size onion, finely chopped

2 medium-size carrots, chopped

1 rib celery, trimmed and chopped

¼ pound fresh fennel (about half a small bulb), tall stalks and leaves discarded and bulb finely chopped

1 medium-size zucchini, trimmed and diced

1 large yellow boiling potato (about ½ pound), such as Yellow Finn or Yukon Gold, peeled and diced

2 cups canned chopped tomatoes, with their juices

4 cups defatted chicken broth, preferably homemade (page 7)

Freshly ground black pepper

¼ cup chopped fresh parsley leaves

A wholesome chicken and vegetable soup that's easy to make with whatever vegetables you have on hand.

▼   ▼   ▼

Heat the oil in a heavy 4-quart saucepan over medium-high heat. Add the chicken, season with salt to taste, and cook, stirring, until all the pieces have turned white and are beginning to brown, about 5 minutes. Remove the chicken with a slotted spoon and place in a small bowl.

Add the onion, carrots, celery, fennel, and zucchini to the pan and cook, stirring, until the vegetables begin to soften, 2 to 3 minutes.

Stir in the chicken pieces, potato, tomatoes, and broth and bring to a boil. Partially cover the saucepan, reduce the heat to medium-low, and simmer until the potato is tender and the chicken cooked through, about 30 minutes. Season with salt and pepper to taste. Stir in the parsley, and serve.

MAKES 6 SERVINGS
Nutritional information per serving
135 calories ▾ 2.5 grams of fat

CHUNKY ROASTED CHICKEN AND VEGETABLE SOUP

▼ ▼

1 medium-size eggplant, unpeeled, ends trimmed, and cut into 1-inch cubes

1 pint cherry tomatoes, cut in half and seeded

1 medium-size onion, cut into 1-inch pieces

½ pound boneless, skinless white-meat chicken, thinly sliced

1 teaspoon olive oil

1 cup canned chopped tomatoes, with their juices

1 large clove garlic, pressed or finely minced

4 cups defatted chicken or vegetable broth, preferably homemade (pages 7, 9)

Freshly ground black pepper

1 tablespoon chopped fresh parsley leaves

1 tablespoon chopped fresh basil leaves

*P*reheat the oven to 450 degrees. Line a medium-size roasting pan with aluminum foil. In the pan, combine the eggplant with the cherry tomatoes, onion, and chicken. Drizzle the olive oil over the vegetables and use a spatula to toss the mixture and distribute the oil. Spread the vegetables in an even layer. Place the roasting pan on the top shelf of the oven and roast until the eggplant is tender and the onion is beginning to brown, about 20 minutes. Remove from the oven and set aside.

Combine the chopped tomatoes with the garlic in a heavy 4-quart saucepan over medium-high heat, season with salt, and cook about 5 minutes. Add the roasted vegetables and the broth and bring to a boil. Reduce the heat to medium-low, partially cover the saucepan, and simmer for 15 minutes. Stir in the parsley and basil, season with salt and pepper to taste, and serve.

MAKES 6 SERVINGS
Nutritional information per serving
111 calories ▾ 2.6 grams of fat

COMFORT CHICKEN SOUP WITH RICE AND SPINACH

▼ ▼

2 teaspoons olive oil

½ pound boneless, skinless white-meat chicken, cut into 1-inch pieces

Salt and freshly ground black pepper

1 medium-size onion, finely chopped

½ cup Arborio or other white short-grain rice

5 cups defatted chicken broth, preferably homemade (page 7)

½ pound fresh spinach leaves, tough stems removed, rinsed well, dried, and roughly chopped to yield about 5 cups

½ teaspoon ground cumin

½ teaspoon ground nutmeg

*N*ourishing and nurturing, this is a marvelous soup for lunch or dinner. Use short-grain rice, such as Arborio or sushi rice.

▼ ▼ ▼

Heat the oil in a heavy 4-quart saucepan over medium-high heat. Add the chicken, season with salt and pepper, and cook, stirring, until the chicken pieces have turned white and are just beginning to brown, about 5 minutes. Remove the chicken and set aside.

Add the onion to the saucepan and cook, stirring, over medium-high heat until it begins to soften, 2 to 3 minutes. Return the chicken to the saucepan, add the rice and broth, and bring to a boil. Reduce the heat to medium-low, partially cover the saucepan, and simmer until the rice is tender, about 20 minutes. Stir in the spinach and continue cooking 5 minutes longer. Add the cumin and nutmeg and stir well to combine. Season with salt and pepper to taste and serve.

NOTE As this soup stands and cools, it thickens; add some broth or water (½ cup at a time) before reheating.

MAKES 6 SERVINGS
Nutritional information per serving
151 calories ▾ 2.4 grams of fat

CHINESE CHICKEN NOODLE SOUP WITH SPINACH AND GINGER

▼ ▼

½ pound angelhair pasta, such as capellini, somen, or other very fine noodles

2 cups fresh spinach leaves, tough stems removed, rinsed well, and shredded

½ pound boneless, skinless white-meat chicken, sliced into 1-inch-wide strips

2 tablespoons sake (Japanese rice wine)

Salt

4 cups defatted Asian Chicken Broth (page 8)

Soy sauce (optional)

1 tablespoon peeled and grated fresh gingerroot

¼ cup thinly sliced scallions, white and green parts

*T*his is real comfort food. Use the skinniest angelhair noodles and add some freshly grated gingerroot at the end.

▼ ▼ ▼

Bring a large pot of water to a boil over high heat. Add the noodles, stir well, and cook until tender, about 5 minutes. Drain, rinse under warm water, drain again, and divide among six individual serving bowls. Add some of the spinach to each bowl (it will wilt from the heat of the noodles). Cover the bowls with plastic wrap to keep warm.

Arrange the strips of chicken on a dinner plate. Sprinkle the rice wine over the strips and season lightly with salt to taste. Cover with plastic wrap or waxed paper and cook in the microwave on high until the chicken strips are cooked through, 2 to 3 minutes. (You can also place the chicken in a vegetable steamer basket over boiling water and cook until the chicken is cooked through, about 5 minutes.)

Meanwhile, pour the broth into a heavy 2-quart saucepan and place over medium-high heat. Simmer until very hot, about 5 minutes. Season with salt or soy sauce to taste. Ladle the broth over the noodles, add about ½ teaspoon of the gingerroot and some of the chicken strips to each serving, and top with the scallions. Serve immediately.

MAKES 6 SERVINGS

Nutritional information per serving

206 calories ▾ 2.0 grams of fat

OLD-FASHIONED
CHICKEN NOODLE SOUP

▼ ▼

1 teaspoon corn or canola oil

½ pound boneless, skinless white-meat chicken, cut into 2-inch pieces

Salt

1 medium-size onion, finely chopped

2 medium-size carrots, chopped

1 rib celery, trimmed and finely chopped

6 cups defatted chicken broth, preferably homemade (page 7)

4 ounces thin spaghetti (spaghettini), broken into thirds

2 tablespoons chopped fresh dill or parsley leaves

Freshly ground black pepper

One of the best soups there is, this chicken soup is almost guaranteed to make you feel better, even if nothing's ailing you. To keep the recipes as low in fat and calories as possible, I've substituted Italian eggless pasta for the more traditional egg noodles. My mother always puts dill in her soup, and it's a flavor that I've come to love. You can substitute parsley for the dill.

▼   ▼   ▼

Heat the oil in a heavy 4-quart saucepan over medium-high heat. Add the chicken, season with salt to taste, and cook, stirring, until the chicken turns white on all sides. Remove the chicken from the saucepan and set aside. To the saucepan add the onion, carrots, and celery and cook, stirring, until the vegetables begin to soften, 2 to 3 minutes. Return the chicken pieces to the saucepan, stir in the broth, and bring to a boil. Reduce the heat to medium-low, partially cover the saucepan, and simmer until the vegetables are tender and the chicken cooked through, about 20 minutes.

Stir in the pasta and turn the heat to medium-high. Cook, stirring occasionally to prevent the pasta from sticking to the bottom of the saucepan, until the pasta is tender, about 10 minutes. Stir in the dill or parsley and season with salt and pepper to taste.

MAKES 6 SERVINGS
Nutritional information per serving
160 calories ▾ 2.8 grams of fat

CHICKEN AND WHITE BEAN SOUP

▼ ▼

1 teaspoon olive oil

½ pound boneless, skinless white-meat chicken, cut into 1-inch pieces

Salt and freshly ground black pepper

1 medium-size onion, finely chopped

2 medium-size carrots, finely chopped

1 rib celery, trimmed and finely chopped

¼ pound fresh fennel (about half a small bulb), tall stalks and leaves discarded and bulb very finely chopped

2 medium-size garlic cloves, pressed or finely minced

2 cups canned chopped tomatoes, with their juices

3 cups defatted chicken or vegetable broth, preferably homemade (pages 7, 9)

2 pinches of red pepper flakes, or more to taste

1 cup cooked or canned (drained and rinsed) white beans, such as Great Northern, cannellini, or navy

¼ cup packed chopped fresh parsley leaves

This is a robust, satisfying soup with aggressive flavors and a lot of hot pepper to spice it up. The finely chopped vegetables give the soup its thick texture. The most efficient way to chop them is to use a food processor; it does the job quickly and easily.

▼ ▼ ▼

Heat the oil in a heavy 4-quart saucepan over medium-high heat. Add the chicken, season with salt and pepper to taste, and cook, stirring, until the chicken pieces have turned white and are just beginning to brown, about 5 minutes. Remove the chicken from the saucepan and set aside.

Add the chopped vegetables to the saucepan and cook over medium-high heat until they begin to soften, 2 to 3 minutes. Stir in the tomatoes, broth, and red pepper flakes, season with salt to taste, and bring to a boil. Partially cover the saucepan, reduce the heat to medium-low, and simmer for about 20 minutes. Add the beans and chicken pieces and cook until the soup is thick and the chicken is cooked through, about 15 minutes longer. Stir in the parsley and serve.

MAKES 6 SERVINGS
Nutritional information per serving
142 calories ▾ 2.4 grams of fat

COUNTRY-STYLE CHICKEN, CORN, AND LIMA BEAN CHOWDER WITH BASIL

▼ ▼

1 teaspoon corn oil

½ pound boneless, skinless
white-meat chicken, cut into
1-inch pieces

1 medium-size onion, finely
chopped

1 serrano chile, seeded and
finely minced

2 cups fresh corn kernels or one
10-ounce package frozen corn
kernels, defrosted but not
cooked

1 large yellow boiling potato
(about ½ pound), such as
Yellow Finn or Yukon Gold,
peeled and diced

4 cups defatted chicken broth,
preferably homemade
(page 7)

Salt and freshly ground black
pepper

2 cups fresh lima beans or one
10-ounce package frozen lima
beans, defrosted but not
cooked

2 tablespoons chopped fresh
basil leaves

A down-home, wholesome soup that makes you think of late summer and farmhouse dinners. But you can make this soup any time of year with frozen corn and limas instead of fresh. Add the lima beans during the last few minutes of cooking so they retain their fresh green color.

▼ ▼ ▼

Heat the oil in a heavy 4-quart saucepan over medium-high heat. Add the chicken pieces and cook, stirring, until the chicken has turned white and is just beginning to brown, about 5 minutes. Remove the chicken from the saucepan and set aside.

Add the onion and chile to the saucepan and cook, stirring, over medium-high heat until the onion begins to soften, 2 to 3 minutes. Stir in the corn, potato, and chicken pieces; add the broth and bring to a boil. Partially cover the saucepan, reduce the heat to medium-low, and simmer until the potato is tender, about 15 minutes. Season with salt and pepper to taste. Stir in the lima beans and cook until they are tender and heated through, about 5 minutes longer. Stir in the basil and serve.

MAKES 6 SERVINGS
Nutritional information per serving
231 calories ▾ 3.1 grams of fat

LOW-FAT CHICKEN SOUP WITH MATZOH BALLS

▼ ▼

½ cup matzoh meal

Salt

2 extra-large eggs

1 extra-large egg white

1 tablespoon carbonated unflavored water

6 cups defatted chicken broth (page 7)

8 pieces carrot reserved from the chicken broth

*E*very year, I prepare the food for our family's Passover dinner.

▼   ▼   ▼

Combine the matzoh meal with salt to taste in a small mixing bowl. In a separate bowl beat the eggs, egg white, and water together until blended. Stir the egg mixture into the matzoh meal with a fork and mix until the mixture is completely moist. Cover the mixing bowl with plastic wrap, place in the refrigerator, and chill for 15 to 30 minutes.

Meanwhile, bring a large pot of water to a boil over high heat. Add salt to taste. When the water is boiling, form the matzoh balls: Wet your hands in cold water and make golf ball–size balls with the matzoh meal-and-egg mixture, drop the matzoh balls into the boiling water, stir to release them if they stick to the bottom of the pot, and boil for 20 to 25 minutes. Remove the matzoh balls from the boiling water with a slotted spoon. The matzoh balls can be added directly to the soup or stored in the refrigerator or freezer. If frozen defrost before adding to the soup.

Heat the broth and carrots in a large saucepan over medium-high heat. Add the matzoh balls. Simmer until the soup is hot and the matzoh balls heated through, 5 to 10 minutes. In each bowl, place a matzoh ball, a piece of carrot, and some broth.

MAKES 8 SERVINGS

Nutritional information per serving

64 calories ▾ 2.0 grams of fat

REAL GUMBO WITH OKRA AND CHICKEN

▼ ▼

1 teaspoon corn or canola oil

½ pound boneless, skinless white-meat chicken, sliced into 1-inch-wide strips

1 large Spanish onion, chopped

1 medium-size green bell pepper, seeded and chopped

2 large cloves garlic, pressed or finely minced

1 pound okra, trimmed and thinly sliced

2 cups canned chopped tomatoes, with their juices

1 bay leaf

1 teaspoon Worcestershire sauce

½ heaping teaspoon cayenne pepper

4 cups defatted chicken broth, preferably homemade (page 7)

Salt and freshly ground black pepper

¼ cup chopped fresh parsley leaves

Tabasco sauce or other hot sauce to taste

*T*his chicken gumbo has all the seasonings, and of course the okra, to make it authentic. It's also very versatile. When served over rice, it's like a stew. To transform it into a seafood soup, add a pound of raw medium-size shrimp, shelled and deveined, in place of the chicken. For added fiery flavor, sprinkle a few drops of Tabasco sauce over each serving.

▼ ▼ ▼

Heat the oil in a heavy 4-quart saucepan over medium-high heat. Add the chicken pieces and cook, stirring, until they have turned white and are just beginning to brown, about 5 minutes. Remove the chicken from the saucepan and set aside. Add the onion, bell pepper, and garlic to the saucepan over medium-high heat, and cook until the vegetables are softened, about 5 minutes. Add the okra, tomatoes, bay leaf, Worcestershire, cayenne, cooked chicken, and broth and season with salt and black pepper to taste. Bring to a boil. Reduce the heat to medium-low, cover the saucepan, and simmer until the chicken is cooked through, about 30 minutes. (If using shrimp, cook the broth 30 minutes, then add the shrimp and cook 5 minutes longer.) Remove the bay leaf, then stir in the parsley. Serve with Tabasco sauce.

MAKES 6 SERVINGS
Nutritional information per serving
120 calories ▾ 2.6 grams of fat

FAR EASTERN FLAVORS

The soups that characterize Asian cooking for me are the light, delicate broth-based soups, with barely cooked vegetables, rice noodles, and seafood—all ethereal yet nourishing, and very satisfying. While Asian cuisines also offer hearty soups that are more like stews, the recipes in this chapter are a sampling of the simple, broth-based soups that preserve the fresh taste of the ingredients.

The following recipes call for Asian-flavored chicken broth. I recommend preparing your own, but you can prepare a short-cut version by simmering 4 cups prepared chicken broth with two slices of fresh gingerroot and a tablespoon of sake (Japanese rice wine) for 15 minutes.

The Asian ingredients asked for in most of these recipes can be found in Asian food markets as well as many large supermarkets.

DASHI WITH SOBA AND SCALLIONS

▼ ▼

6 cups water

2 strips dried kombu

¼ cup bonito flakes

Salt

8 ounces soba noodles

½ cup thinly sliced scallions,
   green and white parts

Dashi is a traditional Japanese broth that's flavored with kombu, a type of seaweed, and bonito flakes. They're steeped in boiling water and strained. Both are available in Asian food markets and health food stores. Soba (buckwheat noodles) are cooked separately, rinsed thoroughly in cold water to remove any starch that may adhere, and added to the soup. The result is an incredibly simple and delicate noodle soup.

▼ ▼ ▼

Heat the water in a heavy 4-quart saucepan until simmering. Turn off the heat. Add the kombu and bonito flakes, cover the saucepan, and allow to stand and steep for 15 minutes. Pour the broth through a fine-mesh sieve and return the liquid to the saucepan. Season with salt to taste.

Meanwhile, bring a separate saucepan of water to boil over high heat. Add the soba and cook, stirring occasionally, until tender, 5 to 7 minutes. Pour the soba into a strainer and rinse thoroughly under warm water. Divide the noodles evenly among six individual serving bowls.

Place the saucepan with the broth over medium-high heat. When the broth is simmering, ladle into the soup bowls over the noodles. Top each serving with a generous portion of the scallions.

MAKES 6 SERVINGS
Nutritional information per serving
142 calories ▾ 0.2 grams of fat.

BUDDHA'S DELIGHT SOUP

▼ ▼

2 quarts water

2 cups small broccoli florets

¼ pound sugar snap or snow
peas (about 1 cup)

1 medium-size carrot, cut into
matchsticks

¼ pound white mushrooms,
sliced

2 cups shredded Chinese
cabbage or bok choy
(both leaves and stems)

one 15-ounce can whole baby
corn, drained (about 2 cups)

½ pound fresh mung bean
sprouts (about 2 cups)

½ pound low-fat tofu, diced

4 ounces cellophane noodles,
soaked in boiling water for
10 minutes, drained

4 cups defatted Asian chicken
broth or vegetable broth,
preferably homemade
(pages 8, 9)

Salt or soy sauce

1 bunch scallions, green and
white parts, very thinly sliced
to yield about 1 cup

This soup was inspired by my daughter Rachel's favorite Chinese restaurant dish, Buddha's delight—a colorful mix of vegetables and tofu in a light sauce. It turns out that vegetables served in broth are every bit as uplifting and very filling too. In this light-tasting soup you parboil or blanch the vegetables first and add them to the hot broth just before serving so they retain their fresh flavor.

▼ ▼ ▼

Bring the water to a boil in a large pot over high heat. Add the broccoli, peas, and carrot and cook for 5 minutes. Use a strainer to remove the vegetables from the pot (leaving the water at a boil), rinse them quickly under cold water, drain, and distribute the vegetables evenly among six small serving bowls.

Next, add the mushrooms, cabbage, corn, and bean sprouts to the boiling water and cook exactly 1 minute. Use a strainer to remove them from the water, rinse quickly under cold water, and drain. Distribute these vegetables among the serving bowls along with the tofu and cellophane noodles.

Heat the broth over medium heat until simmering. Add salt or soy sauce to taste. Spoon approximately ¾ cup of broth into the serving bowls over the vegetables. Garnish with the scallions.

MAKES 6 SERVINGS
Nutritional information per serving
136 calories ▾ 1.3 grams of fat

▼ ▼

2 ounces (1 cup) dried shiitake
mushrooms

2 cups boiling water

4 cups defatted Asian chicken
broth, preferably homemade
(page 8)

1 teaspoon soy sauce, or more
to taste

2 teaspoons corn or canola oil

4 scallions, green and white
parts, minced

1 large clove garlic, pressed or
minced

one 2-inch piece fresh
gingerroot, peeled and minced

½ pound fresh shiitake
mushrooms, stems removed
and caps thinly sliced

½ pound Thai rice noodles

*C*ombine the dried mushrooms with the boiling water in a heat-proof bowl and allow to stand for 30 minutes. Strain the liquid into a small heavy saucepan, reserve the soaked mushrooms for another use, and place the saucepan over medium-high heat. Bring the liquid to a boil and simmer until the liquid is reduced by half, about 10 minutes. Add the broth and soy sauce; simmer over medium heat 10 minutes.

Heat the oil in a heavy 4-quart saucepan over medium-high heat. Add 1 heaping tablespoon of the scallions (reserving the rest for garnish), the garlic and gingerroot and cook, stirring, until the scallions begin to soften, about 1 minute. Stir in the fresh mushrooms and cook until tender, 7 to 10 minutes. Add the broth mixture and cook another 5 minutes.

Meanwhile, bring a large pot of water to a boil over high heat. Add the rice noodles, turn off the heat, and allow to stand, uncovered, until tender, 10 minutes. Drain, rinse under warm water, drain again, and divide among six individual serving bowls. Ladle the mushroom bouillon over the noodles. Garnish with the remaining scallions and serve.

MAKES 6 SERVINGS
Nutritional information per serving
213 calories ▾ 2.2 grams of fat

BLACK MUSHROOM AND SPINACH WONTON SOUP

▼ ▼

1 ounce (½ cup) dried Chinese black or shiitake mushrooms

¼ cup cooked chopped spinach, well drained to remove as much water as possible

2 tablespoons peeled and minced fresh gingerroot

2 tablespoons minced scallions, green and white parts

2 teaspoons soy sauce

1 teaspoon sake (Japanese rice wine)

½ teaspoon toasted sesame oil

1 teaspoon Chinese black vinegar or Worcestershire sauce

1 large egg white

1 teaspoon cornstarch

24 square wonton wrappers

4 cups defatted Asian chicken broth or vegetable broth, preferably homemade (pages 8, 9)

Salt or soy sauce

1 cup well rinsed and shredded fresh spinach leaves, tough stems removed

*T*hese well-flavored wontons make a deliciously low-fat alternative to traditional meat wontons.

▼ ▼ ▼

Place the mushrooms in a small heat-proof bowl, cover with boiling water, and allow to stand for 15 minutes. Drain, discard the water, and squeeze the mushrooms to remove as much water from them as possible. Place in a food processor fitted with the metal blade and process until finely chopped (or chop by hand). You should have about ½ cup chopped mushrooms. Add the cooked spinach, gingerroot, scallions, soy sauce, rice wine, sesame oil, and black vinegar and process just to mix. Add the egg white and cornstarch and pulse the machine on and off to combine.

Place about ½ teaspoon of the wonton filling in the center of a wonton wrapper. Fold the wrapper to enclose the filling, pressing to center the filling, forming a triangle. Starting with the base of the triangle at the bottom, fold the base over on itself, about halfway up the triangle, leaving the peak of the triangle free. Take the two remaining sides of the wrapper and bring them around to touch. Secure them with a dab of water. Place them on a plate or cookie sheet that has been lightly dusted with cornstarch. Repeat until all the wontons are filled.

Bring a large pot of water to a boil over high heat. (If you have a pasta pot with a strainer insert, you should use it; it makes draining the wontons easy.) Drop half the wontons into the boiling water. Stir to make sure they don't stick to the bottom of the pot.

Once they float to the surface, cook for 3 minutes. Drain and repeat with the remaining wontons. Place four wontons in each of six serving bowls.

Meanwhile heat the broth over medium heat until simmering. Season with salt or soy sauce to taste. Spoon the broth over the wontons, garnish with the shredded spinach, and serve.

MAKES 6 SERVINGS
Nutritional information per serving
120 calories ▾ 1.0 grams of fat

CHINESE CABBAGE SOUP WITH CELLOPHANE NOODLES

▼ ▼

2 ounces cellophane noodles

6 cups defatted Asian chicken broth, preferably homemade (page 8)

4 cups Napa cabbage, shredded

2 cups roughly chopped bok choy, leaves and stems

Salt

1 teaspoon toasted sesame oil

This is a low-fat variation of a traditional Chinese cabbage soup, that is fast and easy to make. Cellophane or mung bean noodles are typically sold dry, in two-ounce clusters in bags, and are widely available in most large supermarkets as well as in Asian and specialty food markets.

▼ ▼ ▼

Place the cellophane noodles in a small heat-proof bowl, cover with boiling water, and allow to stand for 15 minutes. Drain and distribute the noodles evenly among six individual serving bowls.

continued

Meanwhile, heat the broth in a heavy 4-quart saucepan over medium-high heat. When the broth boils, add the cabbage and bok choy, reduce the heat to medium-low, and simmer until the cabbage is tender, about 10 minutes. Season with salt to taste and stir in the sesame oil.

Ladle the cabbage soup over the cellophane noodles and serve immediately.

MAKES 6 SERVINGS

Nutritional information per serving
65 calories ▾ 1.7 grams of fat

SUSAN'S MISO SOUP

▼ ▼

6 cups water

4 medium-size dried shiitake
   mushrooms

¼ cup dry bonito flakes

one 6-inch piece dry wakame
   (seaweed), cut with scissors
   into 1-inch pieces

2 tablespoons brown rice miso

4 ounces low-fat tofu, cut into
   1-inch dice

½ cup thinly sliced scallions,
   green and white parts

*S*usan Silver, my sister-in-law, is a superb natural foods cook who learned a lot of what she knows from her days living in a macrobiotic house with Michio and Aveline Kushi. This is her recipe. She uses brown rice miso and advises never to boil the soup after the miso has been added, since the heat will destroy the friendly bacteria in the miso. The bonito flakes and wakame can be found in Asian food markets and health food stores.

▼ ▼ ▼

Combine the water with the mushrooms, bonito flakes, and wakame in a heavy 4-quart saucepan over medium-high heat. Bring the liquid to a boil, reduce the heat to medium-low, and simmer until the mushrooms and wakame are tender, 10 to 15 minutes. Strain the liquid. Discard the bonito flakes. Remove the mushrooms, then stem and thinly slice them. Return the mushrooms and wakame to the saucepan with the liquid and bring the liquid back to a simmer.

Place the miso in a small bowl and add ¼ cup of the soup liquid. Stir with a wire whisk to blend to a smooth paste. Stir the miso into the soup and heat through. Place some of the tofu and scallions in each of the serving bowls. Ladle the soup over the tofu and serve immediately.

MAKES 6 SERVINGS

Nutritional information per serving
30 calories ▾ 0.6 grams of fat

▼ ▼

6 cups cold water

6 dried shiitake mushrooms

2 tablespoons brown rice or red miso

1½ pounds mung bean sprouts (about 6 cups)

4 cups shredded Chinese cabbage or bok choy (both leaves and stems)

4 cups packed fresh spinach leaves, rinsed well, tough stems removed

Salt or soy sauce

½ cup thinly sliced scallions, green and white parts

*M*iso, fermented soybean paste, makes a savory vegetarian broth base for soup. There are dozens of varieties available. The best are prepared in the traditional Japanese method, with organic ingredients and no preservatives or sugar. The miso with the most flavor, and the best for broth and soups, is the darker brown rice or red miso. Lighter miso is more typical of American Japanese restaurants. Miso is best when stirred into a soup just before serving; it should never be boiled.

▼ ▼ ▼

Combine the water and mushrooms in a heavy 4-quart saucepan over medium-high heat and bring to a boil. Reduce the heat to low and simmer until the mushrooms are tender, 10 to 15 minutes. Remove the mushrooms from the liquid, drain, stem, and thinly slice. Strain the liquid to remove any dirt particles. Return the mushrooms to the saucepan with the liquid and bring to a simmer.

Meanwhile, place the miso in a small bowl and add ¼ cup of the mushroom liquid. Use a whisk to create a smooth paste. Set aside.

Add the bean sprouts, cabbage, and spinach to the saucepan with the mushrooms and simmer until the vegetables are tender, 1 to 2 minutes. Turn off the heat. Stir in the miso, add salt or soy sauce to taste, and serve immediately, garnished with the scallions.

MAKES 6 SERVINGS

Nutritional information per serving

59 calories ▾ 0.7 grams of fat

HEARTY
FALL
AND WINTER
SOUPS

There's a veritable wealth of wonderful soups—to warm, to comfort, and to satisfy—you can make with winter vegetables, heartier produce like gnarled celery root and stiff-skinned gourds and squash.

The roots, tubers, and lowly leafy greens—kale, cabbage, and broccoli—of the cold weather harvest may be unappealing to look at or hold, but all are surprisingly subtly flavored when treated with respect and cooked gently to preserve their fresh, distinctive tastes. Carrots, potatoes, yams, and squash provide refined flavors and smooth, luxurious thickening to give many winter soups a rich, creamy texture.

BEET AND FENNEL SOUP WITH
A YOGURT SWIRL

▼ ▼

3 medium-size red beets, greens cut off and reserved for another use, peeled, and diced

1 medium-size onion, diced

½ pound fresh fennel (about 1 small bulb), tall stalks and leaves discarded and bulb cut into 1-inch pieces to yield 2 cups

5 cups cold water

Salt

¼ cup nonfat plain yogurt

*T*he subtle anise flavor of the fennel complements the distinctive beet taste, and the combination is marvelous. As in traditional beet borscht, this soup can be prepared with water rather than broth, and served either hot or cold.

▼ ▼ ▼

Combine the beets, onion, and fennel in a heavy 4-quart saucepan with the water and salt to taste over medium-high heat. Bring to a boil, reduce the heat to medium-low, partially cover the saucepan, and simmer until the beets are tender when pierced with a sharp knife, about 30 minutes.

Transfer the soup to a food processor or blender or use an immersion blender, and process until smooth. Scrape down the sides and process about 15 seconds longer.

Return the soup to the saucepan and reheat before serving. Meanwhile, beat the yogurt with a wire whisk until smooth. Ladle the soup into bowls and drizzle the yogurt on top of each serving in a swirl pattern.

MAKES 6 SERVINGS
Nutritional information per serving
35 calories ▾ 0.2 grams of fat

ROASTED BEET BORSCHT

▼ ▼

4 medium-size red beets (greens removed and reserved for another use), scrubbed

2 medium-size onions, cut in half and thinly sliced

2 cups shredded green cabbage

1 cup canned chopped tomatoes, with their juices

4 cups defatted chicken or vegetable broth, preferably homemade (pages 7, 9)

Kosher salt

¼ teaspoon sour salt (citric acid; see Note), or more to taste, or use 1 tablespoon white vinegar

*W*e have a long tradition of borscht—traditional Russian beet and cabbage soup—in our family. My grandmother prepared a cold beet borscht in the summer (page 159) and a hot meat borscht in the winter. My mother had her own version of meat borscht, made in her pressure cooker, which closely resembled my grandmother's. In this recipe I've tried to capture the character of my mother's borscht. Roasting the beets gives the soup intensity of flavor and color—which more than makes up for the lack of soup bones.

▼ ▼ ▼

Preheat the oven to 450 degrees. Wrap the beets securely in two layers of aluminum foil; place on the middle shelf in the oven and roast for 2 hours. Remove from the oven and unwrap. When the beets are cool enough to handle, use a sharp knife to peel them and cut into 1-inch cubes. Set aside.

In a heavy 4-quart saucepan, combine the beets with the onions, cabbage, tomatoes, and broth, and season with kosher salt to taste. Place over medium-high heat and bring to a boil. Reduce the heat, partially cover the saucepan, and simmer for 1 hour. Add the sour salt and cook 5 minutes longer. Serve in preheated soup bowls.

NOTE Available in the spice/herb section of the supermarket.

MAKES 6 SERVINGS

Nutritional information per serving

55 calories ▾ 0.7 grams of fat

CABBAGE-SOUP-DIET SOUP

▼ ▼

1 small head green cabbage (about 1 pound), shredded

1 medium-size onion, thinly sliced

2 scallions, white and green parts, cut into 1-inch pieces

1 rib celery, trimmed and sliced

½ pound fresh fennel (1 small bulb), tall stalks and leaves discarded and bulb thinly sliced

8 cups water

3 cups canned chopped tomatoes, with their juices

Pinch of red pepper flakes

Salt

¼ cup chopped fresh parsley, basil, or cilantro leaves

I first read about the cabbage soup diet in the newspaper. By the time I received the details of the diet via fax from friends, I had heard about several weight-loss miracles. I don't trust fad diets, no matter who is touting them, but the soup—the mainstay of the diet—actually turned out to be a delicious practically-no-fat chunky vegetable chowder worthy of family and guests alike. I've altered the original recipe, which called for green peppers, and in their place substituted fresh fennel, a flavor I prefer. You can add almost any vegetable to this soup, but potatoes, according to the diet, are strictly forbidden.

▼   ▼   ▼

Combine all the ingredients except the salt and parsley in a heavy 6-quart saucepan over medium-high heat and bring the liquid to a boil. Partially cover the saucepan, reduce the heat to medium-low, and simmer until the vegetables are very tender and the soup has thickened slightly, about 45 minutes. Season with salt to taste, stir in the parsley or other herb, and serve.

MAKES 8 SERVINGS

Nutritional information per serving
48 calories ▾ 0.5 grams of fat

CREAMY CARROT SOUP

▼ ▼

2 teaspoons olive oil

1 medium-size onion, finely
    chopped

1 pound carrots, thinly sliced

⅓ cup Arborio or other short-
    grain white rice

4 cups defatted chicken or
    vegetable broth, preferably
    homemade (pages 7, 9)

Salt and freshly ground black
    pepper

2 tablespoons chopped fresh
    chives

*T*he idea for this soup comes from a French recipe. I changed the original by omitting the crème fraîche, but I found there was nothing missed; this soup tastes incredibly rich anyway. Rice is the secret "creamy" ingredient.

▼ ▼ ▼

Heat the oil in a heavy 4-quart saucepan over medium-high heat. Add the onion and cook, stirring, until it begins to soften, 2 to 3 minutes. Stir in the carrots and cook, stirring, another 2 to 3 minutes. Add the rice and broth and season with salt to taste. Bring to a boil, partially cover the saucepan, and reduce the heat to medium-low. Simmer the soup until the rice is soft and the carrots are tender when pierced with a sharp knife, 25 to 30 minutes.

Transfer the soup to a food processor or blender or use an immersion blender and process until smooth. Scrape down the sides and process a few more seconds. Return the soup to the saucepan and season with salt and pepper to taste. Reheat before serving. Garnish each serving with the chives.

MAKES 6 SERVINGS
Nutritional information per serving
110 calories ▾ 2.1 grams of fat

FENNEL AND BROCCOLI SOUP

▼ ▼

2 teaspoons olive oil

1 large onion, sliced into
¼-inch-thick slices

½ pound fresh fennel (1 small
bulb), tall stalks and leaves
discarded and bulb sliced
¼ inch thick

2 cups broccoli florets

1 medium-size russet or Idaho
potato, peeled and cut into
1-inch cubes

4 cups defatted chicken or
vegetable broth, preferably
homemade (pages 7, 9)

Salt and freshly ground black
pepper

2 tablespoons chopped fresh
dill leaves

The combination of broccoli and fennel create a remarkable flavor. The strong anise taste of fresh fennel mellows considerably when it's cooked, and blends with the broth and broccoli to create a distinctively savory soup. This is a light-textured soup that you can serve throughout the months when fresh fennel is available.

▼ ▼ ▼

Heat the oil in a heavy 4-quart saucepan over medium-high heat. Add the onion, fennel, and broccoli and cook, stirring, until the vegetables begin to soften, 3 to 5 minutes. Add the potato and broth and stir to combine. Increase the heat to high and bring the broth to a boil. Reduce the heat to medium-low, partially cover the saucepan, and simmer until the potatoes, fennel, and broccoli are completely tender and break apart when pierced with a sharp knife, about 20 minutes.

Transfer the soup to a food processor or blender or use an immersion blender, and process until smooth. Season with salt and pepper to taste. Reheat before serving. Garnish each serving with the fresh dill.

MAKES 6 SERVINGS
Nutritional information per serving
74 calories ▾ 2.2 grams of fat

LEAFY KALE AND POTATO SOUP

1 medium-size onion, finely chopped

2 large yellow boiling potatoes (about 1 pound), such as Yellow Finn or Yukon Gold, peeled and diced

4 cups defatted chicken or vegetable broth, preferably homemade (pages 7, 9)

Salt

1 medium-size bunch kale, stems removed, rinsed well, and roughly chopped

Freshly ground black pepper

The taste and texture of kale is distinctive—it's like a heartier version of spinach. A member of the same family as cabbage, kale has a strong and fibrous leaf that doesn't wilt or blend easily, which gives this soup a rough texture. Kale is famously high in vitamins and iron.

▾   ▾   ▾

Combine the onion, potatoes, and broth in a heavy 4-quart saucepan, and place over medium-high heat. Season with salt to taste, and bring to a boil. Reduce the heat to medium-low, cover the saucepan, and simmer until the potato is tender when pierced with a sharp knife, about 20 minutes. Add the kale and stir well to combine. Continue cooking until the kale is tender, 7 to 10 minutes longer.

Transfer the soup to a food processor or blender or use an immersion blender, and process for about 30 seconds. The soup should have some texture and not be completely smooth. Return the soup to the saucepan and season with salt and pepper to taste. Reheat before serving.

MAKES 6 SERVINGS

Nutritional information per serving
89 calories ▾ 1.4 grams of fat

PARSNIP AND POTATO SOUP

▼ ▼

1 medium-size leek, white part only, cut in half lengthwise, rinsed well between the layers, and thinly sliced

2 shallots, chopped to yield about ¼ cup

4 medium-size parsnips (about ½ pound), peeled and chopped

2 large yellow boiling potatoes (about 1 pound), such as Yukon Gold or Yellow Finn, peeled and sliced

4 cups defatted chicken or vegetable broth, preferably homemade (pages 7, 9)

Salt

½ cup chopped fresh chives

1 cup packed fresh parsley leaves

Freshly ground black pepper

*P*arsnips are often added to soups and stews for subtle parsley flavoring, but rarely are they given star billing and allowed to dominate a dish. It's not surprising that so few people actually know what a parsnip tastes like. In this soup there's no mistaking the parsnip's definite parsley-like flavor, which is further enhanced by the fresh parsley that's added at the end. The potato gives the soup its fine creamy texture.

▼ ▼ ▼

Combine the leek, shallots, parsnips, potatoes, and broth in a heavy 4-quart saucepan, and place over high heat. Season with salt to taste, and bring the broth to a boil. Reduce the heat to medium-low, partially cover the saucepan, and simmer until the parsnips and potatoes are tender when pierced with a sharp knife, about 20 minutes. Stir in the chives and parsley and allow to stand for 5 minutes.

Transfer the soup to a food processor or blender or use an immersion blender, and process until smooth. Return the soup to the saucepan. Season with salt and pepper to taste and reheat before serving.

MAKES 6 SERVINGS
Nutritional information per serving
124 calories ▾ 1.6 grams of fat

RUTABAGA AND CELERY ROOT SOUP

▼ ▼

1 medium-size red onion, finely chopped

1 medium-size rutabaga (about 1½ pounds), peeled and cut into 1-inch pieces

1 small celery root (about ½ pound), peeled and cut into 1-inch pieces

¼ teaspoon dried thyme

5 cups defatted chicken or vegetable broth, preferably homemade (pages 7, 9)

Salt and freshly ground black pepper

This is a rich and creamy soup with the distinctive, sharp flavor of the rutabaga (aka yellow turnip) and the subtle celery taste of celeriac, or celery root. Both vegetables require peeling, but a standard kitchen peeler does the job easily.

▼ ▼ ▼

Combine the onion, rutabaga, and celery root in a heavy 4-quart saucepan. Stir in the thyme and broth, place over medium-high heat, and bring the broth to a boil. Reduce the heat to medium-low, partially cover the saucepan, and simmer until the vegetables are tender when pierced with a sharp knife, about 30 minutes.

Transfer the soup to a food processor or blender or use an immersion blender, and process until smooth. Return the soup to the saucepan and season with salt and pepper to taste. Reheat before serving.

MAKES 6 SERVINGS

Nutritional information per serving

85 calories ▾ 1.8 grams of fat

GINGER AND SWEET POTATO SOUP WITH CILANTRO

▼ ▼

2 teaspoons olive oil

1 medium-size leek, white part only, cut in half lengthwise, rinsed well between the layers, and thinly sliced

1 medium-size carrot, chopped

2 pounds sweet potatoes or yams, peeled and cubed

One 1-inch piece fresh gingerroot, peeled and finely chopped, plus 1 teaspoon peeled and grated fresh gingerroot

4 cups defatted chicken or vegetable broth, preferably homemade (pages 7, 9)

Salt

2 tablespoons chopped fresh cilantro leaves

*R*ich and smooth, this luxurious blend of sweet potatoes makes a divine soup. For extra sharp gingery flavor, freshly grated gingerroot is added just before serving.

▼ ▼ ▼

Heat the oil in a heavy 4-quart saucepan over medium-high heat. Add the leek and carrot and cook, stirring, until they begin to soften, 2 to 3 minutes. Stir in the sweet potatoes and chopped gingerroot. Add the broth and bring to a boil. Cover the saucepan, reduce the heat to low, and simmer until the sweet potatoes are soft, about 30 minutes.

Transfer the soup to a food processor or blender or use an immersion blender, and process until smooth. Pour the soup back into the saucepan, adding ½ cup more broth or water if it seems too thick. Season with salt to taste. Reheat before serving. Just before serving, stir in the grated gingerroot and garnish each serving with some of the cilantro.

MAKES 6 SERVINGS

Nutritional information per serving
197 calories ▼ 2.5 grams of fat

TOMATO AND RICE SOUP

2 teaspoons olive oil

1 medium-size onion, finely
chopped

2 medium-size carrots, finely
chopped

¼ pound fresh fennel (about
half a small bulb), tall stalks
and leaves discarded and bulb
finely chopped

1 rib celery, trimmed and finely
chopped

1 cup canned chopped
tomatoes, with their juices

4 cups defatted chicken or
vegetable broth, preferably
homemade (pages 7, 9)

Salt

½ cup short-grain white rice,
preferably Arborio or
Carnaroli (or converted rice)

Freshly ground black pepper

2 tablespoons chopped fresh
parsley leaves

2 tablespoons chopped fresh
basil leaves

This is a light but lusty soup that is very pleasing. My preference is to finely chop the vegetables in a food processor—it gives the finished soup a refined texture—but you can also chop them by hand. For best results, use a short-grain rice, such as Italian Arborio or Carnaroli, that is fairly sturdy and won't become too soft in the soup. Avoid basmati or similar long-grain rice as well as brown rice; they will alter the recipe proportions and timing.

▾   ▾   ▾

Heat the oil in a heavy 4-quart saucepan over medium-high heat. Add the onion, carrots, fennel, and celery and cook, stirring, until they begin to soften, 2 to 3 minutes. Stir in the tomatoes and broth and season with salt to taste. Increase the heat to high and bring to a boil. Reduce the heat to medium-low, partially cover the saucepan, and simmer for 25 to 30 minutes. Stir in the rice and cook until tender, about 20 minutes longer. Season with salt and pepper to taste.

Combine the parsley and basil in a small bowl and garnish each serving with a teaspoon of the mixture.

MAKES 6 SERVINGS
Nutritional information per serving
126 calories ▾ 2.2 grams of fat

WINTER SQUASH SOUP WITH THYME

▼ ▼

2 teaspoons olive oil

1 medium-size onion, finely chopped

2 medium-size carrots, finely chopped

1 rib celery, trimmed and chopped

1 medium-size leek, white part only, cut in half lengthwise, rinsed well between the layers, and thinly sliced

1 pound Hubbard squash, peeled, seeded, and cut into 1-inch cubes

2 sprigs fresh thyme or ¼ teaspoon dried thyme

4 cups defatted chicken or vegetable broth, preferably homemade (pages 7, 9)

Salt and freshly ground black pepper

¼ cup chopped fresh parsley leaves

*T*his sensuous, savory soup has become one of my favorites. You can also use pumpkin, but I like Hubbard squash because it's convenient: widely available in supermarkets already peeled and seeded, and ready to cook.

▼ ▼ ▼

Heat the oil in a heavy 4-quart saucepan over medium-high heat. Add the onion, carrots, celery, and leek and cook, stirring, until they begin to soften, 2 to 3 minutes. Add the squash, thyme, and broth and season with salt to taste. Increase the heat to high and bring to a boil. Reduce the heat to medium-low, partially cover the saucepan, and simmer until the squash is tender when pierced with a sharp knife, about 20 minutes.

Transfer the soup to a food processor or blender or use an immersion blender, and process until smooth. Return the soup to the saucepan and season with pepper to taste. Reheat before serving. Garnish each serving with parsley.

MAKES 6 SERVINGS
Nutritional information per serving
81 calories ▾ 2.5 grams of fat

NOELLE'S SOUP OF WINTER SQUASH AND ROASTED RED PEPPERS

▼ ▼

2 medium-size red bell peppers, cut in half lengthwise, cored and seeded

1¼ pounds Hubbard squash, peeled, seeded, and cubed

1 large onion, finely chopped

4 cups defatted chicken or vegetable broth, preferably homemade (pages 7, 9)

Salt and freshly ground black pepper

*M*y good friend Noelle Blanchard created this successful soup. The texture is perfectly creamy and the subtle sweet bell pepper taste is offset by the bite of delicate black pepper.

▼ ▼ ▼

Preheat the oven broiler. Line a small roasting pan with aluminum foil. Place the pepper halves in the pan, cut side down, and place in the oven on the shelf closest to the broiler. Broil until the pepper skins are completely black, about 8 minutes. Remove from the oven, wrap the peppers in the foil, and allow to stand for 10 minutes. Remove the foil and rub off the blackened skins of the peppers. Slice the peppers into ½-inch-thick strips and set aside.

Combine the squash, onion, and broth in a heavy 4-quart saucepan over medium-high heat and bring to a boil. Partially cover the saucepan, reduce the heat to medium-low, and simmer until the squash is tender when pierced with a sharp knife, about 20 minutes. Add the pepper slices and cook for 5 minutes longer.

Transfer the soup to a food processor or blender or use an immersion blender, and process until smooth. Return the soup to the saucepan, season with salt and a lot of black pepper, and reheat before serving.

MAKES 6 SERVINGS

Nutritional information per serving
72 calories ▾ 1.1 grams of fat

DOUBLE CELERY SOUP

▼ ▼

1 medium-size onion, chopped

6 ribs celery, with leafy tops if possible, trimmed and thinly sliced to yield 2 cups

1 small celery root (about ½ pound), peeled and diced to yield 1 cup

4 cups defatted chicken or vegetable broth, preferably homemade (pages 7, 9)

Salt and freshly ground black pepper

¼ cup chopped fresh chives

*C*elery root, also known as celeriac, and fresh celery infuse this soup with an intense flavor, and create a creamy smooth texture and delicate, pale green color. Watch your salt here, as celery is high in sodium and adds a definite salty taste.

▼   ▼   ▼

Combine the onion, celery, celery root, and broth in a heavy 4-quart saucepan over medium-high heat. When the broth comes to a boil, reduce the heat to medium-low, partially cover the saucepan, and simmer until the celery root is completely tender and breaks apart when pierced with a fork, 20 to 25 minutes.

Transfer the soup to a food processor or blender or use an immersion blender, and process until smooth. Return the soup to the saucepan and season with salt and pepper to taste. Reheat before serving. Garnish each serving with chives.

MAKES 6 SERVINGS

Nutritional information per serving
41 calories ▾ 0.7 grams of fat

ZUPPA!

The tradition of soup in Italy is thousands of years old. Today, every region of Italy has its special preparations as well as variations on the classic soups found throughout the country. Italians have an assortment of names to describe the variety of soups they prepare: *brodo* is the simple broth; *crema* is a creamy pureed soup; *minestra* is a soup in which the ingredients are separate and distinct from the broth in which they are cooked; *zuppa* is a thick soup; and *minestrone* is a particular type of vegetable soup.

Parmigiano-Reggiano is an optional ingredient in many of the recipes. A tablespoon will add about 23 calories and 2 grams of fat. Calorie and fat content of the recipes has been calculated without the addition of cheese.

RIBOLLITA DI TOSCANA

▼ ▼

2 teaspoons olive oil

1 medium-size onion, finely
  chopped

1 medium-size carrot, finely
  chopped

1 rib celery, trimmed and finely
  chopped

2 medium-size cloves garlic,
  pressed or finely minced

1 medium-size russet or Idaho
  potato, peeled and diced

4 cups shredded cabbage

1 bunch green Swiss chard,
  stems removed and leaves
  roughly chopped

2 cups canned chopped
  tomatoes, with their juices

6 cups defatted chicken or
  vegetable broth, preferably
  homemade (pages 7, 9)

2 cups cooked or canned
  (drained and rinsed) small
  white beans, such as Great
  Northern or navy

Salt and freshly ground black
  pepper

½ pound stale Italian bread,
  sliced into ½-inch-thick slices

2 tablespoons freshly grated
  Parmigiano-Reggiano cheese
  (optional)

A classic vegetable and bread soup from Tuscany, where bread, rather than pasta, is the daily starch. The staleness of the bread is important. Fresh bread will almost dissolve into the soup, while day-old bread can hold its own. This soup is best served the day after you prepare it.

▼ ▼ ▼

Heat the oil in a heavy 4-quart saucepan over medium-high heat. Add the onion, carrot, celery, and garlic and cook, stirring, until they begin to soften, 2 to 3 minutes. Add the potato, cabbage, and Swiss chard and continue cooking about 5 minutes longer. Stir in the tomatoes and broth, increase the heat to high, and bring to a boil. Reduce the heat to medium-low, partially cover the saucepan, and simmer for 30 minutes. Add the beans and cook 15 minutes longer. Season with salt and pepper to taste.

Transfer about two thirds of the soup from the saucepan to a large bowl. Arrange half the bread slices over the remaining soup in the pot. Add half the soup from the bowl back into the saucepan to cover the bread. Arrange the remaining bread slices over the soup in the pot and top with the remaining soup. Place the saucepan over medium-low heat, cover, and simmer about 1 hour longer, stirring occasionally to incorporate the bread into the soup.

Allow to cool completely and refrigerate overnight. Reheat, stirring, over medium-low heat. Serve with cheese, if desired.

MAKES 8 SERVINGS
Nutritional information per serving without cheese
206 calories ▼ 2.0 grams of fat

LIGURIAN MINESTRONE

▼ ▼

2 teaspoons olive oil

1 large onion, finely chopped

1 large clove garlic, pressed or finely minced

1 medium-size carrot, finely chopped

1 rib celery, trimmed and finely chopped

1 medium-size russet or Idaho potato, peeled and diced

1 medium-size zucchini, diced

1 cup canned chopped tomatoes, with their juices

4 cups defatted chicken or vegetable broth, preferably homemade (pages 7, 9)

¼ cup short macaroni such as tubetti or ditalini

4 cups packed, thoroughly rinsed, and roughly chopped fresh spinach leaves (about 5 ounces)

½ cup chopped fresh basil leaves

Salt and freshly ground black pepper

2 tablespoons freshly grated Parmigiano-Reggiano cheese (optional)

*E*very region of Italy and practically every town has its own version of what we call *minestrone*, a chunky vegetable soup, made with the typical local ingredients. In this variation the flavors of Liguria, the region of Italy that hugs the part of the northern Mediterranean coastline known as the Italian Riviera, dominate. Liguria is best known as the originator of pesto, and lots of fresh basil is essential in this soup, along with zucchini and fresh spinach.

▼ ▼ ▼

Heat the oil in a heavy 4-quart saucepan over medium-high heat. Add the onion, garlic, carrot, and celery and cook until they begin to soften, 2 to 3 minutes. Add the potato and zucchini and stir well to combine. Stir in the tomatoes and broth, turn the heat to high and bring to a boil. Reduce the heat to medium-low, partially cover the saucepan, and simmer, stirring occasionally, for 30 minutes. Add the macaroni and cook, stirring frequently to prevent it from sticking to the bottom until it is tender, about 10 minutes. Add the spinach and basil, stir well to combine, and cook 5 minutes longer. Season with salt and pepper to taste. Serve with cheese, if desired.

MAKES 6 SERVINGS
Nutritional information per serving without cheese
94 calories ▾ 2.3 grams of fat

▼ ▼

2 teaspoons olive oil

1 medium-size onion, chopped

5 cups defatted chicken or vegetable broth, preferably homemade (pages 7, 9)

½ cup Arborio or other short-grain white rice

1 bunch red Swiss chard, stems removed, well rinsed, and leaves roughly chopped

Salt and freshly ground black pepper

2 tablespoons freshly grated Parmigiano-Reggiano cheese (optional)

*T*his soup is adapted from one of my favorite risotto recipes. Green or red chard can be used in this recipe, or spinach if chard is not available. This is a quick, comforting, and very satisfying soup.

▼ ▼ ▼

Heat the oil in a heavy 4-quart saucepan over medium-high heat. Add the onion and cook, stirring, until it begins to soften, 2 to 3 minutes. Add the broth and bring to a boil. Stir in the rice, partially cover the saucepan, reduce the heat to medium-low, and simmer, stirring occasionally to prevent the rice from sticking to the bottom, until the rice is tender, about 20 minutes. Stir in the chard, increase the heat to medium-high, and cook until the chard is tender, about 5 minutes longer. Season with salt and pepper to taste. Ladle into bowls and serve with cheese if desired.

MAKES 6 SERVINGS
Nutritional information per serving without cheese
118 calories ▼ 2.2 grams of fat

ZUPPA OF FUSILLI AND POTATO

▼ ▼

1 teaspoon olive oil

1 large onion, finely chopped

2 medium-size carrots, finely chopped

2 medium-size ribs celery, trimmed and finely chopped

1 medium-size clove garlic, pressed or finely minced

1 medium-size yellow boiling potato, such as Yukon Gold or Yellow Finn, peeled, cut into quarters, and thinly sliced

¼ cup tomato paste

Pinch of red pepper flakes

6 cups defatted chicken or vegetable broth, preferably homemade (pages 7, 9)

2 cups water

½ pound fusilli or other short twisted pasta

Salt and freshly ground black pepper

2 tablespoons chopped fresh parsley leaves

2 tablespoons chopped fresh basil leaves

2 tablespoons freshly grated Parmigiano-Reggiano cheese (optional)

*W*arming, filling, and hearty, this soup is a meal in itself that you can serve as a main course with a salad and some good, crusty bread. A lot of liquid is called for because the pasta absorbs so much while it cooks. You may need to add some additional broth or water if you don't serve the soup as soon as it's finished cooking; as it stands the pasta continues to absorb liquid.

▼ ▼ ▼

Heat the oil in a heavy 4-quart saucepan over medium-high heat. Add the onion, carrots, celery, and garlic and cook, stirring, until they begin to soften, 2 to 3 minutes. Stir in the potato, tomato paste, pepper flakes, broth, and water. Bring to a boil, cover the saucepan, reduce the heat to medium-low, and simmer until the potato is falling-apart tender, 20 to 25 minutes. Increase the heat to medium-high, add the fusilli, and cook, stirring frequently, until the pasta is tender but firm (al dente), about 10 minutes. Season with salt and pepper to taste, then stir in the parsley and basil. Serve with cheese, if desired.

MAKES 6 SERVINGS
Nutritional information per serving without cheese
207 calories ▾ 2.3 grams of fat

MINESTRA OF SQUASH AND RICE WITH SAGE

▼ ▼

2 teaspoons olive oil

1 medium-size onion, finely
chopped

1 medium-size carrot, finely
chopped

1 rib celery, trimmed and finely
chopped

1 pound Hubbard squash,
peeled, seeded, and cut into
½-inch dice

4 cups defatted chicken or
vegetable broth, preferably
homemade (pages 7, 9)

½ cup Arborio or other short-
grain white rice

Salt and freshly ground black
pepper

2 tablespoons chopped fresh
parsley leaves

1 large sage leaf, finely chopped
to yield 1 teaspoon

𝒯his is a traditional soup from Lombardy, where rice, squash, called *zucca* in Italian, and sage are standard ingredients. Sage gives the soup its distinctive, aromatic flavor. It's best to serve this soup as soon as it's cooked; as it stands, the rice becomes overcooked and soft.

▼ ▼ ▼

Heat the oil in a heavy 4-quart saucepan over medium-high heat. Add the onion, carrot, celery, and squash and cook, stirring, until they begin to soften, 2 to 3 minutes. Add the broth and bring to a boil. Stir in the rice and cook, stirring frequently to keep it from sticking to the pan, until the rice and squash are tender, about 20 minutes. Season with salt and pepper to taste. Stir in the parsley and sage and serve immediately.

MAKES 6 SERVINGS
Nutritional information per serving
129 calories ▾ 2.3 grams of fat

MINESTRA OF BROCCOLI AND PASTA

▼ ▼

1 small head broccoflower, or
   1 pound cauliflower or
   broccoli, cut into smallest
   florets to yield about 3 cups

2 teaspoons olive oil

1 medium-size clove garlic,
   pressed or finely minced

2 tablespoons tomato paste

2 cups defatted chicken or
   vegetable broth, preferably
   homemade (pages 7, 9)

½ pound spaghetti or linguine,
   broken into 2-inch pieces
   (do not use spaghettini or
   capellini; they are too fine for
   this soup)

Salt and freshly ground black
   pepper

¼ cup chopped fresh parsley
   leaves

*T*his is a Roman soup traditionally prepared with broth made from skate (ray fish) wings. The Italian recipe calls for broccoli *romanesco*, a vegetable that tastes like a cross between cauliflower and broccoli, and more subtly flavored than either one. It's close to broccoflower, which can be bought at some specialty grocers. You can use broccoli, cauliflower, or the broccoflower, whichever is available. This satisfying soup can be served, as it is in Italy, as a first course, or as a light main course.

▼ ▼ ▼

Place the broccoflower florets in a steamer basket over boiling water and steam until tender when pierced with a sharp knife, 5 to 7 minutes. Rinse under cold water to stop the cooking, drain, and set aside. Reserve the steaming water.

Heat the oil in a heavy 4-quart saucepan over medium-high heat. Add the garlic and tomato paste and cook, stirring, 2 to 3 minutes. Add the broth and the reserved cooking liquid, stirring well. Bring to a boil and cook for 5 minutes. Add the spaghetti and cook, stirring frequently, until the pasta is tender but firm (al dente), 7 to 10 minutes. Add the broccoflower and cook until it is heated through, 3 to 5 minutes longer. Season with salt and pepper to taste, stir in the parsley, and serve.

MAKES 6 SERVINGS
Nutritional information per serving
198 calories ▾ 2.7 grams of fat

ZUPPA OF BROWN LENTILS AND ARUGULA

▼ ▼

2 teaspoons olive oil

1 medium-size onion, finely chopped

1 large clove garlic, pressed or finely minced

2 cups dried small lentils, preferably Italian brown lentils from Castelluccio or the French green lentils du Puy, picked over and rinsed

4 cups defatted chicken or vegetable broth, preferably homemade (pages 7, 9)

2 cups water

1 bunch arugula, stems removed, leaves rinsed well, dried, and roughly chopped to yield about 4 cups

Salt and freshly ground black pepper

The sharp taste of the arugula nicely offsets the the richness of the lentils. You can substitute spinach for the arugula.

▼ ▼ ▼

Heat the oil in a heavy 4-quart saucepan over medium-high heat. Add the onion and garlic and cook, stirring, until the onion begins to soften, 2 to 3 minutes. Add the lentils, broth, and water and bring to a boil. Partially cover the saucepan, reduce the heat to medium-low, and simmer until the lentils are tender and the soup has thickened, about 45 minutes. Stir in the arugula and cook 5 minutes longer. Season with salt and pepper to taste and serve.

MAKES 6 SERVINGS

Nutritional information per serving
230 calories ▾ 2.7 grams of fat

ZUPPA OF FARRO WITH TOMATOES AND SPINACH

▼ ▼

1 teaspoon olive oil

1 medium-size onion, finely
chopped

2 medium-size carrots, finely
chopped

1 rib celery, trimmed and finely
chopped

2 cups canned chopped
tomatoes, with their juices

4 cups defatted chicken or
vegetable broth, preferably
homemade (pages 7, 9)

1 cup farro

4 cups loosely packed, rinsed,
and roughly chopped fresh
spinach leaves

Salt and freshly ground black
pepper

2 tablespoons freshly grated
Parmigiano-Reggiano cheese
(optional)

This hearty, savory soup is made with a particular variety of whole wheat that the Italians call farro. It cooks into a luscious, creamy consistency very much like barley. Other whole wheat berries don't compare; they require much more cooking time and never become so exquisitely textured. Farro can be purchased in Italian specialty stores. If you can't find it, pearl barley is the best substitute. As this soup stands, it thickens, so you may want to add some extra broth before you reheat it.

▼ ▼ ▼

Heat the oil in a heavy 4-quart saucepan over medium-high heat. Add the onion, carrots, and celery and cook, stirring, until the onion begins to soften, 2 to 3 minutes. Add the tomatoes and broth and stir in the farro. Bring to a boil, reduce the heat to medium-low, cover the saucepan, and simmer until the farro is tender and the grains are enlarged and have turned a creamy, light color, about 30 minutes. Stir in the spinach and cook until the spinach is tender, about 5 minutes longer. Season with salt and pepper to taste. Garnish each serving with some cheese, if desired.

MAKES 6 SERVINGS
Nutritional information per serving without cheese
163 calories ▼ 2.5 grams of fat

PAPPA AL POMODORO

▾ ▾

¾ cups stale country-style bread cubes (about ½ pound) with crust

4 cups warm defatted vegetable broth, preferably homemade (page 9)

1 teaspoon olive oil

2 large cloves garlic, finely minced

3 pounds ripe plum tomatoes, cored and coarsely chopped

Salt

1 cup packed fresh basil leaves, coarsely chopped

A pappa is a mush or baby food in Italian. This thick soup of bread, juicy, ripe tomatoes, and fragrant basil is one of the great summer treats to enjoy when you're in Tuscany. Use only the ripest tomatoes and good, crusty, country-style stale bread. If possible use bread that's unsalted, which is most like the bread of Tuscany, and preferably not sourdough. This soup is served at room temperature.

▾ ▾ ▾

Place the bread cubes and broth in a medium-size mixing bowl, stir to combine, and set aside.

Meanwhile, heat the oil in a heavy 4-quart saucepan over medium-high heat. Add the garlic and cook, stirring, about 1 minute. Add the tomatoes, season with salt to taste, and cook, stirring frequently, until the tomatoes are soft and have the consistency of a chunky sauce, 10 to 15 minutes. Stir in the basil and cook until the basil is tender and combined with the tomatoes, 3 to 5 minutes longer. Pour the tomato-and-basil mixture into the mixing bowl with the bread and broth and stir to combine. Allow to cool, uncovered, to room temperature. Taste and season with more salt if necessary. Stir again before serving.

MAKES 6 SERVINGS
Nutritional information per serving
110 calories ▾ 3.0 grams of fat

Maybe it's the daffodils and crocus, popping through the snow, that make me rush out and buy asparagus. Or maybe it's just that after a long winter, like those we have here in the Northeast, I'm looking forward to new taste sensations. Once spring is around the corner, I turn to the fresh, delicate, and very green flavors it brings with it: asparagus, peas, young lettuce, and, above all, leeks. These tastes and more are captured in these glorious, simple spring soups.

Serve these soups as an elegant first course or as a main course at lunch. Spring never tasted so good.

ARTICHOKE AND SUNCHOKE CHOWDER

▼ ▼

2 teaspoons olive oil

1 medium-size onion, finely chopped

1 large clove garlic, pressed or finely minced

Pinch of red pepper flakes, or more to taste

10-ounce package frozen artichoke hearts, defrosted

2 pounds sunchokes (Jerusalem artichokes), peeled and cut into 2-inch pieces

4 cups defatted chicken or vegetable broth, preferably homemade (pages 7, 9)

1 cup fresh parsley leaves, chopped

Salt

*W*ith artichokes available all year long, you can make this soup whenever you like, but for me, artichokes are still a spring rite. This chunky blend of sunchokes (Jerusalem artichokes), the tuberous root of a sunflower variety, and artichoke hearts makes a wonderfully savory soup. Use lots of garlic and hot red pepper for a strong assertive flavor. This soup should have a coarse, chunky texture.

▼ ▼ ▼

Heat the oil in a heavy 4-quart saucepan over medium-high heat. Add the onion and garlic and cook, stirring, until the onion begins to soften, 2 to 3 minutes. Add the red pepper flakes, artichoke hearts, and sunchokes. Stir in the broth and bring to a boil. Partially cover the saucepan, reduce the heat to medium-low, and simmer until the sunchokes are tender, 15 to 20 minutes.

Transfer the soup to a food processor with the parsley. Pulse the machine on and off three or four times just until the mixture is coarsely chopped, not pureed. Return the soup to the saucepan, season with salt to taste, and reheat before serving.

MAKES 6 SERVINGS

Nutritional information per serving

170 calories ▾ 2.3 grams of fat

ASPARAGUS AND BABY PEA POTAGE WITH TARRAGON

▼ ▼

2 teaspoons olive oil

1 large Vidalia or Spanish onion (about 1 pound), coarsely chopped

1 large shallot, chopped

4 cups defatted chicken or vegetable broth, preferably homemade (pages 7, 9)

1 pound medium-size asparagus spears, tough bottoms cut off and discarded, spears peeled about two thirds of the way to the tip, and cut into 1-inch pieces

2 cups shelled fresh peas or one 10-ounce package frozen peas, defrosted

½ cup packed fresh tarragon leaves

Salt and freshly ground black pepper

The ultimate spring soup—made with asparagus, baby peas, and tarragon leaves. Fresh peas are super sweet for only a short time after they're picked; like corn, they become more starchy than sweet the longer they're stored. Use frozen baby peas if the freshest peas are not available. Use fresh, not dried, tarragon leaves, pulled from the stems, for the best flavor.

▼ ▼ ▼

Heat the oil in a heavy 4-quart saucepan over medium-high heat. Add the onion and shallot and cook, stirring, until the onion begins to soften, 2 to 3 minutes. Add the broth, increase the heat to high, and bring the liquid to a boil. Cover the saucepan, reduce the heat to medium-low, and simmer until the onion is tender, about 10 minutes. Add the asparagus and peas and cook until the asparagus is tender when pierced with a sharp knife, 5 to 7 minutes. Stir in the tarragon.

Transfer the soup to a food processor or blender or use an immersion blender, and process until smooth. Return the soup to the saucepan, season with salt and pepper to taste, and gently reheat before serving.

MAKES 6 SERVINGS
Nutritional information per serving
108 calories ▾ 2.4 grams of fat

SPRING ASPARAGUS SOUP

▼ ▼

2 teaspoons olive oil

1 large Spanish onion, coarsely chopped

1 medium-size Idaho potato, peeled and cut into 2-inch pieces

4 cups defatted chicken or vegetable broth, preferably homemade (pages 7, 9)

3 pounds medium-size asparagus spears, tough bottoms cut off and discarded, spears peeled about two thirds of the way to the tip and cut into 1-inch pieces

Salt and freshly ground black pepper

*T*his simple blended-smooth soup is a delightful way to enjoy the best springtime asparagus. Use thicker spears if possible; the asparagus needs to be peeled before cooking and skinny spears are difficult to peel. It's best to serve this soup as soon as it's been prepared to retain its delicate light green color and flavor; as this soup stands or is reheated it will turn a darker shade of green and the flavor will intensify.

▼ ▼ ▼

Heat the oil in a heavy 4-quart saucepan over medium-high heat. Add the onion and cook, stirring, until it begins to soften, 2 to 3 minutes. Add the potato and broth, increase the heat to high, and bring the liquid to a boil. Cover the saucepan, reduce the heat to medium-low, and simmer until the potato breaks apart easily when pierced with a fork, about 20 minutes. Add the asparagus and cook 5 minutes longer.

Transfer the soup to a food processor or blender or use an immersion blender, and process until smooth. Return the soup to the saucepan, season with salt and pepper to taste, and gently reheat before serving.

MAKES 6 SERVINGS
Nutritional information per serving
77 calories ▾ 2.4 grams of fat

ARUGULA VICHYSSOISE

▾ ▾

2 teaspoons olive oil

2 medium-size onions, coarsely chopped

2 medium-size leeks, white part only, cut in half lengthwise, rinsed well between the layers, and thickly sliced

1 medium-size Idaho potato, peeled and cubed

4 cups defatted chicken or vegetable broth, preferably homemade (pages 7, 9)

2 bunches arugula, well rinsed and coarsely chopped to yield 6 cups, or 2 bunches watercress, thickest stems cut off and discarded

Salt and freshly ground black pepper

2 tablespoons chopped fresh chives

*L*ight and low-fat, this soup has all the extravagance and richness of the classic vichyssoise, but none of the fat. Although vichyssoise sounds like it originated in France, it was actually created in America by a French chef. Today the name refers to almost any soup made with puree of leek and potato. Be sure to rinse the arugula well before chopping, since it tends to be sandy. You can prepare this soup with watercress in place of the arugula.

▾ ▾ ▾

Heat the oil in a heavy 4-quart saucepan over medium-high heat. Add the onions and leeks and cook, stirring, until the onions begin to soften, 2 to 3 minutes. Add the potato and broth, increase the heat to high, and bring the liquid to a boil. Cover the saucepan, reduce the heat to medium-low, and simmer until the potato breaks apart easily when pierced with a fork, about 20 minutes. Add the arugula and cook 5 minutes longer.

Transfer the soup to a food processor or blender or use an immersion blender, and process until smooth. Season with salt and pepper to taste. Serve hot or cold, each serving garnished with the chives.

MAKES 6 SERVINGS

Nutritional information per serving

73 calories ▾ 2.3 grams of fat

VELVETY LEEK SOUP

▼ ▼

2 teaspoons olive oil

*3 pounds leeks, white part
only, cut in half lengthwise,
rinsed well between the
layers, and thickly sliced*

*1 large yellow boiling potato
(about ½ pound), preferably
Yukon Gold or Yellow Finn,
peeled and cut into 1-inch
pieces*

*4 cups defatted chicken or
vegetable broth, preferably
homemade (pages 7, 9)*

*Salt and freshly ground white
pepper*

*U*nlike traditional leek and potato soups, this one is almost all leek with only a small amount of potato to provide a creamy, sensuous consistency. The leek flavor is very pronounced.

▼ ▼ ▼

Heat the oil in a heavy 4-quart saucepan over medium-high heat. Add the leeks and cook, stirring, until they begin to soften, 2 to 3 minutes. Add the potato and broth and bring to a boil. Reduce the heat to low, cover the saucepan, and simmer until the leeks and potato are tender when pierced with a sharp knife, 20 to 25 minutes.

Transfer the soup to a food processor or blender or use an immersion blender, and process until smooth. Return the soup to the saucepan, season with salt to taste, reheat, and garnish each serving with a pinch of white pepper.

MAKES 6 SERVINGS
Nutritional information per serving
125 calories ▾ 2.5 grams of fat

LUSTY LEEK AND POTATO SOUP

▼ ▼

1 tablespoon olive oil

2 medium-size leeks, white part only, cut in half lengthwise, rinsed well between the layers, and very thinly sliced to yield 4 cups

2 pounds yellow boiling potatoes, such as Yukon Gold or Yellow Finn, peeled, cut in half, and thinly sliced to yield 4 to 5 cups

4 cups defatted chicken or vegetable broth, preferably homemade (pages 7, 9)

Salt and freshly ground black pepper

A simple unrefined soup that always pleases. This is one of those great combinations of ingredients that never fails. Slice the leeks and potatoes very thin; it gives this soup a rich, full texture.

▼ ▼ ▼

Heat the oil in a heavy 4-quart saucepan over medium-high heat. Add the leeks and cook, stirring, until they begin to soften, 2 to 3 minutes. Stir in the potatoes and broth and bring to a boil. Cover the saucepan, reduce the heat to medium-low, and simmer until the vegetables are tender, 20 to 25 minutes. Season with salt and pepper to taste and serve.

MAKES 6 SERVINGS
Nutritional information per serving
196 calories ▾ 2.9 grams of fat

TENDER LETTUCE SOUP WITH CHERVIL AND CHIVES

▼ ▼

2 teaspoons olive oil

2 medium-size onions, finely chopped

1 medium-size Idaho potato, peeled and cut into 2-inch pieces

4 cups defatted chicken or vegetable broth, preferably homemade (pages 7, 9)

2 medium-size heads Boston lettuce, heads cored, leaves rinsed and dried, and roughly chopped (to yield about 10 cups)

Salt and freshly ground black pepper

2 tablespoons chopped fresh chives

2 tablespoons chopped fresh chervil or parsley leaves

*T*he soft, buttery leaves of Boston lettuce make a delicate sensual soup. Although this soup is blended, it never becomes completely smooth, retaining some of the leafy texture of the lettuce. The herbs are meant as a garnish, but they add a lot of flavor to this otherwise subtle soup. If chervil is not available, use parsley.

▼ ▼ ▼

Heat the oil in a heavy 4-quart saucepan over medium-high heat. Add the onions and cook, stirring, until they begin to soften, 2 to 3 minutes. Add the potato and broth, increase the heat to high, and bring the liquid to a boil. Cover the saucepan, reduce the heat to medium-low, and simmer until the potato breaks apart easily when pierced with a sharp knife, about 20 minutes. Add the lettuce and stir to combine with the broth-and-onion mixture. Allow to cook 5 minutes longer.

Transfer the soup to a food processor or blender or use an immersion blender, and process until smooth. Return the soup to the saucepan, season with salt and pepper to taste, and gently reheat before serving. Garnish each serving with chives and chervil.

MAKES 6 SERVINGS
Nutritional information per serving
68 calories ▾ 2.3 grams of fat

VIDALIA ONION SOUP

▼ ▼

1 teaspoon olive oil

3 to 4 large Vidalia onions
(about 4 pounds), cut in half,
and thinly sliced

½ cup dry white wine

5 cups defatted chicken or
vegetable broth, preferably
homemade (pages 7, 9)

Salt and freshly ground black
pepper

Six ¼-inch-thick slices French
bread

3 tablespoons freshly grated
Parmigiano-Reggiano cheese

This delicious soup made with the spring crop of native Georgia Vidalia onions gets its intensity of flavor from the sweetness of the onions, which are cooked slowly for a long time until they are a rich caramel color. You may have to cook the onions in two batches; even though they will cook down a lot, the quantity of onions at the beginning is a lot for even the biggest pan. Use Spanish onions if Vidalias are not available.

▼ ▼ ▼

Heat the oil in a large skillet, preferably one with a nonstick surface, over medium heat. Add the onions and cook, stirring occasionally, until the onions are golden brown, 45 minutes to 1 hour. Transfer the onions to a heavy 4-quart saucepan. Add the wine to the saucepan in which the onions were cooked and deglaze the pan over medium-high heat, stirring, until the wine is reduced by half, 3 to 5 minutes. Pour the wine into the saucepan with the onions. Add the broth, increase the heat to medium-high, and bring to a boil. Reduce the heat to medium-low, cover the saucepan, and simmer until the flavors are combined, about 15 minutes. Season with salt and pepper to taste.

While the soup is cooking, toast the slices of bread. Serve the soup in individual soup bowls. Top each serving with a piece of toast and a sprinkling of cheese.

MAKES 6 SERVINGS
Nutritional information per serving
188 calories ▾ 3.0 grams of fat

POTATO POTAGE PARMENTIER

▼ ▼

2 teaspoons olive oil

1 medium-size onion, chopped

2 medium-size carrots, chopped

1 rib celery, trimmed and
chopped

1 leek, white part only, cut in
half lengthwise, rinsed well
between the layers, and very
thinly sliced to yield 4 cups

3 medium-size (about 1 pound)
yellow boiling potatoes,
preferably Yukon Gold or
Yellow Finn, peeled and
cubed

5 cups chicken or vegetable
broth, preferably homemade
(pages 7, 9)

Salt and freshly ground black
pepper

As a young eater, I had a limited taste for French food. A reliable and almost always available choice in restaurants was a simple *potage* of potatoes, leeks, onions, and carrots that was pureed with no cream added. It remains one of my favorite soups.

▼ ▼ ▼

Heat the oil in a 4-quart heavy saucepan over medium-high heat. Add the onion, carrots, celery, and leek and cook, stirring, until the vegetables begin to soften, 2 to 3 minutes. Add the potatoes and broth and bring the liquid to a boil. Reduce the heat to medium-low and simmer until the potatoes are tender when pierced with a sharp knife, about 20 minutes.

Transfer the soup to a food processor or blender or use an immersion blender, and process until smooth. Return the soup to the saucepan, season with salt and pepper to taste, and place the pan over low heat. When the soup is hot, serve.

MAKES 6 SERVINGS

Nutritional information per serving
108 calories ▾ 2.2 grams of fat

CREAMY WATERCRESS SOUP

▼ ▼

2 teaspoons olive oil

1 medium-size onion, finely chopped

1 rib celery, trimmed and sliced

2 large yellow boiling potatoes (about 1 pound), preferably Yukon Gold or Yellow Finn, peeled and cut into medium-size dice

2 cups cold water

2 cups skim milk

1 bunch watercress, rinsed and drained, 6 sprigs reserved for garnish

Salt and freshly ground black pepper

*A*dapted from a traditional French recipe, this watercress soup is made with milk and no broth. It is delectably creamy and very satisfying. Even the watercress-wary will embrace it.

▼   ▼   ▼

Heat the oil in a heavy 4-quart saucepan over medium-high heat. Add the onion and celery and cook, stirring, until the onion begins to soften, 2 to 3 minutes. Add the potatoes and stir well to combine. Add the water and milk, increase the heat to medium-high, and bring to a boil. Watch carefully because the milk has a tendency to boil over. Immediately reduce the heat to medium-low, partially cover the saucepan, and simmer until the potatoes are falling-apart tender, 20 to 25 minutes. Add the watercress and cook 5 minutes longer.

Transfer the soup to a food processor or blender or use an immersion blender, and process until smooth. Season with salt and pepper to taste and return the soup to the saucepan. Reheat before serving. Garnish each serving with a sprig of watercress.

MAKES 6 SERVINGS
Nutritional information per serving
108 calories ▾ 1.8 grams of fat

SOUPS
THAT ZING!

Hot and spicy flavors add zest and great taste to soup, and help to make up for the missing flavor of fat. These low-fat soups are all pungently spicy, but still mellow enough to allow you to taste the other flavors. Although you'll find more soups throughout the book that are enhanced with some hot pepper—whether it's fresh green chiles, dry pepper flakes, or Tabasco sauce—this selection has some extra forceful spark that makes these soups stand out and zing.

PICANTE PEPPER BISQUE

▾ ▾

1 medium-size green bell
   pepper, seeded and diced

3 medium-size red bell peppers,
   seeded and diced

1 fresh jalapeño or serrano
   chile, seeded and chopped

1 large onion, finely chopped

Pinch of hot paprika

½ cup cooked basmati rice

4 cups defatted chicken or
   vegetable broth, preferably
   homemade (pages 7, 9)

1 tablespoon red wine vinegar

Salt

A mix of sweet and hot peppers makes this soup delectably peppery. Use green and red bell peppers and one very hot jalapeño or serrano chile to make the soup powerfully *picante* (hot), as they say in Spanish. Remember to wash your hands, knife, and cutting board after working with the hot chile pepper.

▾ ▾ ▾

Combine the peppers, chile, onion, paprika, rice, and broth in a heavy 4-quart saucepan over medium-high heat and bring to a boil. Reduce the heat to medium-low, partially cover the saucepan, and simmer until the vegetables and rice are completely tender, 20 to 25 minutes.

Transfer the soup to a food processor or blender or use an immersion blender, and process until smooth. Stir in the vinegar and season with salt to taste. Return the soup to the saucepan, place over medium-low heat, and reheat before serving.

MAKES 6 SERVINGS

Nutritional information per serving
101 calories ▾ 0.9 grams of fat

CURRIED CAULIFLOWER SOUP

▾ ▾

2 teaspoons olive oil

1 large onion, finely chopped

1 teaspoon curry powder, or
   more to taste

1 medium-size head
   cauliflower, cut into small
   florets

1 medium-size clove garlic,
   chopped

3 cups cold water

Salt

1 cup skim milk

Freshly ground black pepper

¼ cup chopped fresh chives

6 tablespoons nonfat sour
   cream

*C*urry and cauliflower make a perfect flavor combination. Pureed cauliflower is surprisingly light, smooth, and very creamy. The result is a delicate but luxurious soup. A note on curry: Curry powder is typically a blend of many spices and can vary from mild to quite hot. Know your curry's power and add it accordingly. The sour cream elevates the presentation and adds a cool contrast to the curry.

▾ ▾ ▾

Heat the oil in a heavy 4-quart saucepan over medium-high heat. Add the onion and cook, stirring, until it begins to soften, 2 to 3 minutes. Add the curry powder, stirring constantly (so as not to burn it) for 1 minute. Add the cauliflower, garlic, water, and salt to taste. Increase the heat to high and bring to a boil. Reduce the heat to medium-low, cover the saucepan, and simmer until the cauliflower is completely tender and breaks apart easily when pierced with a sharp knife, about 20 minutes. Add the milk, bring back to a simmer, and remove from the heat.

Transfer the soup to a food processor or blender or use an immersion blender, and process until smooth. Return the soup to the saucepan, season with salt and pepper to taste, and reheat over low heat before serving. Garnish each serving with some chives and a tablespoon of sour cream.

MAKES 6 SERVINGS

Nutritional information per serving
89 calories ▾ 2.3 grams of fat

SPICY CAULIFLOWER AND POTATO SOUP

▼ ▼

1 medium-size onion, finely chopped

2 medium-size carrots, chopped

1 rib celery, trimmed and chopped

1 medium-size yellow boiling potato, such as Yellow Finn or Yukon Gold, peeled and diced

2 cups cauliflower florets

Pinch of red pepper flakes

5 cups defatted chicken or vegetable broth, preferably homemade (pages 7, 9)

Salt

2 tablespoons chopped fresh parsley leaves

*C*auliflower can magically give a soup a luxurious, creamy consistency. This is a tangy and very tasty soup with a great, sensuous texture. The cauliflower flavor is discreet.

▼ ▼ ▼

Combine the onion, carrots, celery, potato, cauliflower, red pepper flakes, broth, and salt to taste in a heavy 4-quart saucepan over medium-high heat and bring to a boil. Reduce the heat to medium-low, partially cover the saucepan, and simmer until the potato and cauliflower are tender when pierced with a sharp knife, about 20 minutes.

Transfer the soup to a food processor or blender or use an immersion blender, and process until smooth. Return the soup to the saucepan, season with salt to taste, and reheat before serving. Garnish each serving with the parsley.

MAKES 6 SERVINGS
Nutritional information per serving
61 calories ▾ 1.6 grams of fat

SPICY RED MUSSEL SOUP

▼ ▼

5 pounds fresh mussels,
  scrubbed and debearded
  (discard any broken shells)

2 cups dry white wine

2 cups cold water

1 teaspoon olive oil

2 large cloves garlic, pressed or
  finely minced

3 cups canned chopped
  tomatoes, with their juices

Pinch of red pepper flakes

¼ cup chopped fresh parsley
  leaves

*I*ntensely flavorful and quite piquant, this is a deliciously hearty soup. I like to use farmed mussels because they're a lot cleaner than wild mussels and don't leave a sandy residue in the broth.

▼　▼　▼

Place the mussels in a heavy 8-quart stockpot. Pour in the wine and water, cover the pot, and place over medium-high heat. Cook until all the mussels are open, about 5 minutes. Let stand to cool slightly, about 5 minutes longer. Discard any unopened mussels. Reserve about 18 mussels in their shells, place in a small bowl, and cover with aluminum foil to keep warm. Remove the remaining mussels from their shells and set aside. Return the pot to the stove over medium-high heat. Cook the liquid in the pot until it is reduced by half, about 10 minutes. Strain the liquid and set aside.

In a heavy 4-quart saucepan heat the oil over medium-high heat. Add the garlic and cook, stirring, about 1 minute. Add the tomatoes, red pepper flakes, and the reduced mussel liquid. Reduce the heat to medium-low, and cook about 20 minutes to combine the flavors. Add the shelled mussels and simmer to heat the mussels through, 3 to 5 minutes longer. Stir in the parsley. To serve, ladle the mussel soup into individual serving bowls and garnish with the reserved mussels.

MAKES 6 SERVINGS
Nutritional information per serving
153 calories ▾ 2.8 grams of fat

SUMMER SALSA SOUP WITH TOMATOES, BLACK BEANS, AND CORN

▼ ▼

2 pounds ripe tomatoes, cored
and cut into chunks

1 medium-size yellow onion,
quartered

1 serrano or jalapeño chile,
seeded

¼ cup fresh cilantro leaves

Salt

1 cup freshly cooked or canned
(drained and rinsed) black
beans

1 cup cooked corn kernels

12 baked fat-free tortilla chips

*T*his is an easy soup to make in the summer when corn and tomatoes are at their best. Use canned black beans for convenience—just be sure to rinse them well and drain thoroughly before adding them to the soup.

▼   ▼   ▼

Combine the tomatoes, onion, chile, and cilantro leaves in a food processor or blender and process until very finely chopped, and not quite smooth. Season with salt to taste. Transfer the soup to a large mixing bowl and stir in the black beans and corn. Refrigerate until cold, at least 1 hour. Taste the soup and add more salt if necessary. Garnish each serving with 2 tortilla chips.

MAKES 6 SERVINGS
Nutritional information per serving
126 calories ▾ 1.2 grams of fat

RACY RED LENTIL SOUP

▼ ▼

2 teaspoons olive oil

1 medium-size onion, finely chopped

1 tablespoon peeled and grated fresh gingerroot

1 large clove garlic, pressed or finely minced

Pinch of fennel seeds

Pinch of cumin seeds

¼ teaspoon red pepper flakes

1 cup dried red lentils, picked over and rinsed

5 cups defatted chicken or vegetable broth, preferably homemade (pages 7, 9)

Salt

*D*elicately laced with cumin, fennel, and hot red pepper, this red lentil soup is spicy, and very tasty. Red lentils have an altogether different flavor than brown lentils, but don't be wary—they're every bit as delicious. I like to puree this soup to give it a creamy consistency.

▼ ▼ ▼

Heat the oil in a heavy 4-quart saucepan over medium-high heat. Add the onion, gingerroot, garlic, fennel and cumin seeds, and red pepper flakes and cook, stirring, until the onion begins to soften, 2 to 3 minutes. Add the lentils and broth and bring to a boil. Reduce the heat to medium-low, cover the saucepan, and simmer until the lentils are soft and the soup is thick, 45 minutes to 1 hour.

Transfer about half the soup to a food processor or blender and process until smooth. Return the blended soup to the saucepan and stir well to combine with the unblended soup. Add salt to taste.

MAKES 6 SERVINGS
Nutritional information per serving
134 calories ▾ 2.4 grams of fat

TANGY TOMATO AND CHICKPEA SOUP

▼ ▼ ▼ ▼ ▼ ▼ ▼ ▼ ▼ ▼ ▼ ▼ ▼ ▼ ▼ ▼ ▼ ▼ ▼ ▼

1 teaspoon olive oil

1 medium-size onion, finely
chopped

⅛ teaspoon red pepper flakes,
or more to taste

2 cups canned chopped
tomatoes, with their juices

4 cups defatted chicken or
vegetable broth, preferably
homemade (pages 7, 9)

2 cups cooked or canned
(drained and rinsed)
chickpeas

Salt

2 tablespoons chopped fresh
parsley leaves

*T*his is a lively and simple soup. You can tone it down or liven it up by adjusting the amount of red pepper flakes.

▼ ▼ ▼

Heat the oil in a heavy 4-quart saucepan over medium-high heat. Add the onion and cook, stirring, until it begins to soften, 2 to 3 minutes. Add the red pepper flakes, tomatoes, and broth and bring to a boil. Reduce the heat to medium-low, cover the saucepan, and simmer for 20 minutes.

Transfer the soup to a food processor or blender or use an immersion blender, and process until smooth, about 30 seconds. Scrape down the sides and process a few seconds longer.

Return the soup to the saucepan over medium-high heat. Add the chickpeas and cook until the chickpeas are heated through and the flavors are well combined, about 10 minutes longer. Season with salt to taste, stir in the parsley, and serve.

MAKES 6 SERVINGS
Nutritional information per serving
132 calories ▾ 2.9 grams of fat

SUMMER'S BOUNTY

One of my favorite times of the year to cook is when farm stands and produce shelves are overflowing with the summer harvest. Even in the midst of scorching heat, when the bounty arrives in my kitchen, I love to prepare soups with garden-grown tomatoes and herbs, farm-fresh greens, and sun-soaked veggies. Some of these soups are served hot; most are well-chilled. But whether hot or cold, spicy or subtle, these savory summer soups are a perfect first course or light entree for a breezy, easy summer meal.

Some tips to keep in mind when preparing cold soups:

- Always refrigerate cold soups for at least 30 minutes and up to 3 hours after you prepare them to give the flavors an opportunity to marry and to allow the soup to become sufficiently cold (the ideal serving temperature is 40 degrees).
- Always check the seasonings just before you serve a cold, savory soup. Colder foods tend to have less flavor than warmer foods; you may want to add more salt and pepper.
- Finally, I like to chill my soup bowls in the refrigerator to make sure that when I serve a well-chilled soup it's as deliciously cold, invigorating, and refreshing as possible.

COOL CUCUMBER AND YOGURT SOUP

▼ ▼

2 pounds cucumbers, peeled,
  cut in half lengthwise, seeded
  and sliced ½ inch thick

Salt

2 medium-size scallions, white
  part only, cut into 1-inch
  pieces

1 large clove garlic, or more to
  taste

2 cups nonfat plain yogurt

2 tablespoons chopped fresh dill
  or mint leaves

*I*nspired by the classic Eastern *raita* and the Middle Eastern *cacik*, this cucumber soup gets a lot of flavor from the scallions and garlic, which lend a pleasant sharpness. For best results, use pickling cucumbers, or the foot-long English cucumbers. These have fewer and smaller seeds and are less watery. Since you generously salt the cucumbers before combining them into the soup, you may not need to salt the soup again. Be sure to taste before serving.

▼ ▼ ▼

Place the cucumbers in a colander, sprinkle liberally with salt, and allow to stand and drain 30 minutes or longer. Use a paper towel to blot dry the cucumbers and transfer them to a food processor or blender. Add the scallions and garlic and process until smooth. Add the yogurt and process until the soup is smooth and uniformly pale green in color, about 30 seconds longer. Refrigerate until thoroughly chilled, at least 30 minutes. Serve in chilled bowls. Top each serving with a sprinkling of dill or mint.

MAKES 6 SERVINGS

Nutritional information per serving

67 calories ▼ 0.4 grams of fat

CHILLED CORN VICHYSSOISE

▼ ▼

2 teaspoons olive oil

2 large shallots, chopped

1 medium-size leek, white part
only, cut in half lengthwise,
rinsed well between the
layers, and thinly sliced

2 large yellow boiling potatoes
(about 1 pound), preferably
Yukon Gold or Yellow Finn,
peeled and diced

4 cups defatted chicken or
vegetable broth, preferably
homemade (pages 7, 9)

2 cups fresh corn kernels or one
10-ounce package frozen
corn, defrosted

1 cup buttermilk

Salt and freshly ground black
pepper

½ teaspoon ground cumin

2 tablespoons chopped fresh
chives

*T*his creamy, cold corn-leek-and-potato soup has a wonderfully pronounced corn flavor that's heightened by the cumin. Buttermilk adds some richness.

▼ ▼ ▼

Heat the oil in a heavy 4-quart saucepan over medium-high heat. Add the shallots and leek and cook, stirring, until they begin to soften, 2 to 3 minutes. Stir in the potatoes and cook about 1 minute longer. Add the broth and bring to a boil. Reduce the heat to medium-low, cover the saucepan, and simmer until the potato is tender, about 20 minutes. Add the corn and cook until the corn is tender, about 5 minutes longer.

Transfer the soup to a food processor or blender, or use an immersion blender, and process until smooth. Pour into a large mixing bowl and allow to come to room temperature. Refrigerate until thoroughly chilled. Stir in the buttermilk, season with salt and a lot of black pepper, add the cumin, and garnish each serving with some chives.

MAKES 6 SERVINGS
Nutritional information per serving
164 calories ▾ 2.8 grams of fat

CORN AND CHILE CHOWDER

▼ ▼

1 teaspoon corn or canola oil

1 medium-size onion, finely
   chopped

1 green serrano chile, seeded
   and minced

1 pound yellow boiling
   potatoes, such as Yukon Gold
   or Yellow Finn, peeled and
   cut into ½-inch dice

4 cups defatted chicken or
   vegetable broth, preferably
   homemade (pages 7, 9)

3 cups fresh corn kernels or one
   10-ounce package frozen
   corn, defrosted

2 tablespoons chopped fresh
   cilantro leaves

½ medium-size red bell pepper,
   seeded and finely diced

A hot soup for a rainy August day, this soup could almost be a meal—the potatoes and corn are so satisfying. Hot chile pepper gives a boost of flavor that really complements the corn. If you prefer a milder flavor, omit the serrano chile and substitute a sweet green bell pepper in its place.

▼ ▼ ▼

Heat the oil in a heavy 4-quart saucepan over medium-high heat. Add the onion and chile and cook, stirring, until the onion begins to soften, 2 to 3 minutes. Add the potatoes and broth, increase the heat to high, and bring to a boil. Reduce the heat to medium-low, cover the saucepan, and simmer until the potatoes are tender when pierced with a sharp knife, about 20 minutes. Add the corn and cook 5 minutes longer. Remove from the heat. Stir in the cilantro and red pepper and ladle into individual soup bowls.

MAKES 6 SERVINGS

Nutritional information per serving
177 calories ▾ 2.4 grams of fat

THE BEST GAZPACHO

3 medium-size ripe tomatoes
   (about 2 pounds), seeded and
   cut into chunks

1 large cucumber, peeled, cut
   in half lengthwise, seeded,
   and cut into 1-inch pieces

1 medium-size red bell pepper,
   seeded and cut into 1-inch
   pieces

1 scallion, white and green
   parts, cut into 1-inch pieces

1 small clove garlic

1 tablespoon red wine vinegar

½ cup tomato juice

Salt and freshly ground black
   pepper

I have been preparing this gazpacho for as long as I have been cooking. Really ripe tomatoes are essential to this soup. I have prepared it with both green and red bell peppers, and I usually prefer the red because the color of the finished soup is brighter, but the flavor is not much different so you can use whatever is convenient. You can also add more garlic if you like; I find a small clove provides a subtle but good taste. You can add garnishes to this soup to make it more substantial: chopped cucumber, chopped onion, or croutons.

▾   ▾   ▾

Combine the tomatoes, cucumber, bell pepper, scallion, and garlic in a food processor or blender and process until smooth. Add the vinegar and tomato juice and continue processing until thoroughly combined with the vegetable puree. Transfer the soup to a bowl and season with salt and pepper to taste. Refrigerate until thoroughly chilled. Check the seasonings before serving. Serve in chilled bowls.

MAKES 6 SERVINGS
Nutritional information per serving
48 calories ▾ 0.6 grams of fat

PROVENÇAL VEGETABLE SOUP

▼ ▼

1 small eggplant (about
  1 pound), left unpeeled,
  and cubed

2 medium-size zucchini, cubed

Salt

2 teaspoons olive oil

1 medium-size onion, finely
  chopped

1 large clove garlic, pressed or
  finely minced

1 medium-size red bell pepper,
  seeded and coarsely chopped

1 cup canned chopped
  tomatoes, with their juices

4 cups defatted chicken or
  vegetable broth, preferably
  homemade (pages 7, 9)

¼ cup chopped fresh basil
  leaves

2 tablespoons chopped fresh
  parsley leaves

Freshly ground black pepper

*W*ith all the ingredients of a ratatouille, this soup has a robust taste. While you can also serve this soup in its chunky state, when pureed it becomes more refined and has a surprisingly creamy texture that comes from the eggplant.

▼ ▼ ▼

Combine the eggplant and zucchini in a large colander, sprinkle liberally with salt, toss, and allow to stand and drain for 30 minutes.

Heat the oil in a heavy 4-quart saucepan over medium-high heat. Add the onion and garlic and cook, stirring, until the onion begins to soften, 2 to 3 minutes. Add the eggplant, zucchini, and red pepper and stir well to combine. Continue cooking, stirring occasionally, until the zucchini and eggplant begin to lose their raw appearance, 3 to 5 minutes longer. Add the tomatoes and broth, stir to combine, and increase the heat to high. When the liquid comes to a boil, reduce the heat to medium-low, partially cover the saucepan, and simmer until the vegetables are completely tender, 20 to 30 minutes. Stir in 2 tablespoons of the basil and parsley and cook 5 minutes longer.

Transfer the soup to a food processor or blender or use an immersion blender, and process until smooth. Season with salt and pepper to taste and reheat before serving. Garnish each serving with the remaining 2 tablespoons basil.

MAKES 6 SERVINGS

Nutritional information per serving
77 calories ▾ 2.3 grams of fat

ZUCCHINI AND BASIL SOUP

▼ ▼

2 medium-size zucchini (about 1 pound), ends trimmed and cut into 1-inch pieces

1 medium-size onion, peeled and thinly sliced

4 cups defatted chicken or vegetable broth, preferably homemade (pages 7, 9)

Salt and freshly ground black pepper

¼ cup packed chopped fresh basil leaves

*T*his is a quick, easy and invigorating soup to make and has no added fat. It's a great way to use up those big, overgrown zucchini. You can serve it hot or cold.

▼ ▼ ▼

Combine the zucchini, onion, and broth in a heavy 4-quart saucepan over medium-high heat. Season with salt to taste. When the broth comes to a boil, reduce the heat to medium-low, partially cover the saucepan, and simmer until the vegetables are completely tender, about 20 minutes.

Transfer the soup in batches to a food processor or blender or use an immersion blender, and process until smooth. Return the soup to the saucepan, season with salt and pepper to taste, and reheat. Garnish with chopped basil before serving.

MAKES 6 SERVINGS
Nutritional information per serving
29 calories ▾ 0.5 grams of fat

SPLENDID SPINACH AND FENNEL SOUP WITH BASIL

▼ ▼

1 pound fresh fennel (about 1 medium-size bulb), tall stalks and leaves discarded and bulb cut into 1-inch pieces

1 medium-size onion, chopped

1 large yellow boiling potato (about ½ pound), such as Yukon Gold or Yellow Finn, peeled and diced

4 cups defatted chicken or vegetable broth, preferably homemade (pages 7, 9)

One 10-ounce package fresh spinach, tough stems removed, rinsed well, dried, and roughly chopped

1 cup packed fresh basil leaves

Salt

This soup has a very lively, distinctive spinach taste, especially when you prepare it with fresh organic leaf spinach. Any fresh spinach will do, just be sure to remove the stems and rinse it well before cooking.

▼ ▼ ▼

Combine the fennel, onion, potato, and broth in a heavy 4-quart saucepan over medium-high heat. Bring to a boil, partially cover the pan, reduce the heat to medium-low, and simmer until the potato and fennel are tender when pierced with a sharp knife, about 20 minutes. Stir in the spinach and basil and cook 5 minutes longer.

Transfer the soup to a food processor or blender or use an immersion blender, and process until smooth. Pour the soup into a large bowl and allow to come to room temperature. Cover and refrigerate until thoroughly chilled. Season with salt to taste and serve.

MAKES 6 SERVINGS
Nutritional information per serving
82 calories ▾ 0.8 grams of fat

SUMMER SQUASH SOUP WITH FRESH HERBS

▼ ▼

2 pounds yellow summer squash, cut into 1-inch-thick slices

4 cups defatted chicken or vegetable broth, preferably homemade (pages 7, 9)

¼ cup chopped fresh herbs, preferably a combination of marjoram, parsley, basil, and chives

Salt and freshly ground black pepper

This is a superb soup with energetic flavor that will surely surprise you—summer squash takes on a completely new dimension of flavor when prepared this way. I like to use a combination of fresh herbs for a strong, convincing herb taste. You can also use just one herb for a singular herb presence.

▼ ▼ ▼

Combine the squash and broth in a heavy 4-quart saucepan over medium-high heat and bring to a boil. Reduce the heat to low, partially cover the saucepan, and simmer until the squash is completely tender when pierced with a sharp knife, 15 to 20 minutes.

Transfer the squash-and-broth mixture to a food processor or blender or use an immersion blender, and process until smooth. Add the herbs and process about 15 seconds longer to combine with the soup. Pour the soup into a bowl, season with salt and pepper to taste, and allow to cool to room temperature. Cover the bowl and refrigerate until thoroughly chilled. Taste and check the seasonings; serve in chilled bowls.

MAKES 6 SERVINGS
Nutritional information per serving
39 calories ▾ 0.9 grams of fat

CREAMY TOMATO BISQUE WITH SHALLOTS AND TARRAGON

▼ ▼

2 teaspoons olive oil

4 large shallots (about ¼ pound), chopped

1 large Spanish onion, chopped

3 pints (3 pounds) cherry tomatoes, seeded

¼ cup uncooked Arborio, or other short-grain white rice

4 cups defatted chicken or vegetable broth, preferably homemade (pages 7, 9)

½ cup packed fresh tarragon leaves, or use fresh basil leaves

Salt and freshly ground black pepper

*T*he recipe for this soup was given to me years ago by a friend and great cook, Katrina Hall. Use the sweetest summer cherry tomatoes in this soup, which can be served cold or hot. I strongly recommend using fresh rather than dried tarragon—it gives the best taste and a delicate aroma. You can also use fresh basil.

▼ ▼ ▼

Heat the oil in a heavy 4-quart saucepan over medium-high heat. Add the shallots and onion and cook, stirring, until they begin to soften, 2 to 3 minutes. Add the tomatoes, rice, broth, and tarragon and bring to a boil. Reduce the heat to medium-low, cover the saucepan, and simmer 15 to 20 minutes, until the rice is tender.

Transfer the soup to a food processor or blender or use an immersion blender and process until smooth. Season with salt and pepper to taste. If serving cold, cool to room temperature, then refrigerate until the soup is thoroughly chilled. Taste and add more salt and pepper if necessary before serving.

MAKES 6 SERVINGS
Nutritional information per serving
133 calories ▾ 1.6 grams of fat

ROASTED CHERRY TOMATO AND FENNEL SOUP WITH BASIL

▼ ▼

1 pint cherry tomatoes, cut in half and seeded

½ pound fresh fennel (about 1 small bulb), tall stalks and leaves discarded and bulb cut into 2-inch pieces

1 medium-size onion, cut into 2-inch pieces

2 teaspoons olive oil

4 cups defatted chicken or vegetable broth, preferably homemade (pages 7, 9)

¼ cup packed fresh basil leaves

Salt

*T*his soup is light yet full-flavored. Roasting the vegetables gives them an intense taste.

▼ ▼ ▼

Preheat the oven to 450 degrees. Line a small roasting pan with aluminum foil.

Combine the tomatoes, fennel, and onion in the pan. Drizzle the oil over the vegetables and toss with a spatula to coat them. Place on the top shelf in the oven and roast until the fennel is tender when pierced with a sharp knife and the tomatoes are beginning to turn brown, 15 to 20 minutes.

Use a spoon to transfer the vegetables to a heavy 4-quart saucepan. Stir in the broth and bring to a boil over medium-high heat. Cover, reduce the heat to medium-low, and simmer for 10 minutes. Add the basil and cook 5 minutes longer.

Transfer the vegetables from the soup to a food processor or blender or use an immersion blender, and process until smooth. Pour the vegetable puree back into the soup and stir to combine. Season with salt to taste. Reheat before serving.

MAKES 6 SERVINGS

Nutritional information per serving
61 calories ▾ 2.3 grams of fat

MIDSUMMER VEGETABLE CHOWDER

▼ ▼

2 teaspoons olive oil

2 medium-size onions, finely chopped

4 medium-size carrots, cut in half lengthwise, and sliced ½ inch thick

4 medium-size red or yellow potatoes, peeled and diced

2 medium-size zucchini, cut in half lengthwise, and sliced

1 medium-size yellow squash, cut in half lengthwise and sliced

2 pounds ripe tomatoes, peeled, seeded, and chopped, with their juices (or use 3 cups canned)

4 cups defatted chicken or vegetable broth, preferably homemade (pages 7, 9)

Salt and freshly ground black pepper

2 cups cooked or canned (drained and rinsed) small white beans, such as Great Northern, cannellini, or navy

4 tablespoons chopped fresh herbs, such as parsley, basil, or marjoram

2 tablespoons freshly grated Parmigiano-Reggiano cheese (optional)

This fresh-tasting soup should cook only as long as the vegetables require, 20 to 30 minutes. You can make it any time of year, but it's most fun to prepare it in the summer, when you can pick up the vegetables at a farm stand, come home, and quickly cook up a potful. It's good hot or cold. The Parmigiano-Reggiano cheese is optional.

▼ ▼ ▼

Heat the oil in a heavy 6-quart saucepan over medium-high heat. Add the onions and carrots and cook, stirring, until the onion begins to soften, 2 to 3 minutes. Stir in the potatoes, zucchini, yellow squash, and tomatoes. Add the broth, season with salt and pepper to taste, and cover the saucepan. Increase the heat to high and bring to a boil. Reduce the heat to low and simmer until the potatoes are tender, about 20 minutes. Add the beans and cook, stirring occasionally, about 10 minutes longer to heat through. Stir in the parsley and basil. Garnish each serving with the cheese, if desired.

MAKES 6 SERVINGS
Nutritional information per serving without cheese
298 calories ▾ 2.5 grams of fat

ROASTED YELLOW PEPPER SOUP

▼ ▼

4 medium-size yellow bell
  peppers, cut in half and
  seeded

1 large onion, finely chopped

1 clove garlic, pressed or finely
  minced

1 medium-size yellow boiling
  potato (about ½ pound),
  such as Yukon Gold or Yellow
  Finn, peeled and diced

4 cups defatted chicken or
  vegetable broth, preferably
  homemade (pages 7, 9)

Salt and freshly ground black
  pepper

1 fresh jalapeño chile, seeded
  and minced

*T*he first time I tasted yellow pepper soup was in Florence at the restaurant Cibreo. My attempts to re-create that extraordinary flavor have resulted in a variety of recipes. This version uses roasted peppers to give even more intense pepper flavor.

▼   ▼   ▼

Preheat the oven broiler. Line a small roasting pan with aluminum foil. Place the pepper halves cut side down in the pan and place in the oven on the shelf closest to the broiler. Broil until the pepper skins are completely black, about 8 minutes. Remove from the oven, wrap the peppers in the foil, and allow to stand for 10 minutes. Remove the foil and rub the blackened skins from the peppers. Cut the peppers into 1-inch pieces.

Combine the peppers, onion, garlic, potato, and broth in a heavy 4-quart saucepan over medium-high heat and bring to a boil. Reduce the heat to medium-low, partially cover the saucepan, and simmer until the potato is completely tender, 15 to 20 minutes.

Transfer the soup to a food processor or blender or use an immersion blender, and process until smooth. Return the soup to the saucepan, season with salt and pepper to taste, and reheat over medium-low heat before serving. Garnish each serving with ¼ teaspoon of the jalapeño.

MAKES 6 SERVINGS

Nutritional information per serving
80 calories ▾ 0.7 grams of fat

SUMMER WATERCRESS SOUP

▼ ▼

2 medium-size bunches
   watercress, stems removed,
   rinsed, and dried

1 medium-size onion, peeled
   and cut into 1-inch pieces

1 large yellow boiling potato,
   (about ½ pound), such as
   Yukon Gold or Yellow Finn,
   peeled and diced

1 medium-size clove garlic,
   peeled

2 cups water

Salt and freshly ground black
   pepper

2 cups buttermilk

*I*n the summer, a regular soup at my grandmother's house was *schav*, or cold sorrel soup. I never enjoyed the bitter taste of the sorrel when I was young but I've come to really love bitter greens like sorrel, arugula, and watercress. Because sorrel is available for only a brief period in the early spring, this version with watercress can be prepared all year long, or all summer long. This is a light soup. The buttermilk adds tang and richness.

▼ ▼ ▼

Combine the watercress, onion, potato, garlic, and water in a heavy 4-quart saucepan over medium-high heat. Bring to a boil, partially cover the saucepan, reduce the heat to medium-low, and simmer until the potato is tender, 20 to 25 minutes. Transfer the soup to a food processor or blender or use an immersion blender, process until smooth, then season with salt and pepper to taste. Pour the soup into a large mixing bowl and allow it to come to room temperature. Cover the bowl, refrigerate until the soup is thoroughly chilled, about 3 hours. Stir in the buttermilk before serving.

MAKES 6 SERVINGS

Nutritional information per serving
67 calories ▾ 0.1 grams of fat

NANNY'S BEET BORSCHT

▼ ▼

4 medium-size beets, greens cut off and reserved for another use, peeled, and diced

1 medium-size onion, diced

5 cups cold water

Salt

3 small red potatoes, boiled in water to cover until tender, peeled, and cut in half

1 medium-size cucumber, preferably pickling or English, peeled, seeded, and diced

6 tablespoons nonfat plain yogurt or nonfat sour cream

*M*y grandmother always served this soup to us in the summer, garnished with boiled potato, chopped cucumber, and a hefty dollop of sour cream. I have substituted nonfat yogurt for the sour cream; you can also use nonfat sour cream. This soup, in keeping with the kosher tradition, is prepared with water rather than broth, so it can be served with either a meat- or milk-based meal.

▼ ▼ ▼

Combine the beets, onion, water, and salt to taste in a heavy 4-quart saucepan over medium-high heat. Bring to a boil, reduce the heat to medium-low, partially cover the saucepan, and simmer until the beets are tender when pierced with a sharp knife, about 30 minutes. Remove from the heat and allow to cool to room temperature.

Transfer the soup to a food processor or blender or use an immersion blender, and process until smooth. Pour the soup into a bowl, cover, and allow to come to room temperature. Refrigerate until thoroughly chilled. Season with more salt to taste if necessary. Top each serving with half a potato, some cucumber, and a tablespoon of yogurt or sour cream.

MAKES 6 SERVINGS

Nutritional information per serving

70 calories ▼ 0.2 grams of fat

FAST
AND FRESH
FRUIT SOUPS

Like a sorbet or fruit salad, an icy bowl of a refreshing fruit soup is the perfect, light ending to any meal. Of course, if your taste runs to sweet before a meal, you can also serve these soups as a first course.

HONEYDEW AND LIME SOUP

▼ ▼

1 medium-size ripe honeydew melon, peeled, seeded, and cut into chunks

Juice and grated zest of 1 lime

¼ cup granulated sugar, or as needed

½ cup nonfat plain yogurt

The delicate taste of honeydew melon is given a boost in this soup with a hefty dose of lime juice and lime zest. Nonfat yogurt helps to smooth out the coarse texture of pureed honeydew to make the consistency creamy. To choose a ripe honeydew, hold the melon up to your nose at the stem end. You should be able to detect a distinct but mild honeydew fragrance. If the smell is strong, the melon is probably overripe.

▼ ▼ ▼

Combine the melon, lime juice and zest, and sugar in a food processor or blender and process until smooth. Taste the mixture and add more sugar, 1 teaspoon at a time, if desired. Add the yogurt and process just long enough to combine. Transfer to a mixing bowl, cover, and refrigerate until thoroughly chilled. Stir well and serve in chilled bowls.

MAKES 6 SERVINGS

Nutritional information per serving
133 calories ▾ 0.3 grams of fat

SUMMER FRUIT "MINESTRONE"

▼ ▼

2 cups orange juice

¼ cup granulated sugar

¼ cup fresh lemon juice
  (from 1 lemon)

3 ripe peaches, pitted and
  roughly chopped to yield
  2 cups

3 ripe nectarines, pitted and
  roughly chopped to yield
  2 cups

4 ripe red plums, such as Santa
  Rosa, pitted and roughly
  chopped to yield 2 cups

1 cup fresh blueberries, picked
  over, stems removed, and
  rinsed

12 fresh mint leaves

A chunky fruit soup, this melange of berries, peaches, nectarines, and plums resembles a minestrone in texture only. It's enticingly sweet and fragrantly flavorful.

▼   ▼   ▼

Combine the orange juice, sugar, and lemon juice in a large mixing bowl and stir to dissolve the sugar. Add the peaches, nectarines, and plums and stir to combine. Refrigerate until cold, at least 1 hour. Stir in the blueberries. Serve in chilled bowls, each serving garnished with two mint leaves.

MAKES 6 SERVINGS
Nutritional information per serving
162 calories ▼ 0.9 grams of fat

CANTALOUPE AND MINT SOUP WITH LEMON

▼ ▼

4 pounds ripe cantaloupe (about 2 whole melons) peeled, seeded, and cut into chunks

¼ cup packed fresh mint leaves

¼ cup fresh lemon juice (from 1 lemon)

2 tablespoons granulated sugar, or more to taste

*C*antaloupe becomes thick and lusciously creamy when pureed. I like to add the mint to the melon before it's pureed for a sprinkling of green color and hint of flavor. If you prefer, you can add the mint, chopped, as a garnish on each serving. The sugar and lemon juice combine to bring out the best of the melon flavor, but you may have to make some adjustments with these two flavorings since melons vary in sweetness and may call for more sugar or less lemon juice; use your palate to decide.

▼ ▼ ▼

Combine the cantaloupe, mint, lemon juice, and sugar in a food processor or blender and process until smooth. Taste and add more sugar or lemon juice if desired. Refrigerate until thoroughly chilled. Stir well and serve in chilled bowls.

MAKES 6 SERVINGS
Nutritional information per serving
87 calories ▼ 0.6 grams of fat

VERY BERRY SOUP

▼ ▼

1 quart fresh blueberries, picked over, stems removed, and rinsed

½ cup granulated sugar

2 tablespoons water

1 pint fresh raspberries, picked over

¼ cup nonfat plain yogurt

This makes a refreshing but sweetly satisfying dessert. You can substitute strawberries and blackberries in this recipe.

▼ ▼ ▼

Combine the blueberries with the sugar and water in a heavy 4-quart saucepan, preferably one with a nonstick surface, over medium-high heat. Cook, stirring, until the sugar dissolves and the mixture begins to bubble. Reduce the heat to low and simmer, stirring occasionally, until the mixture is thickened and deep blue, about 10 minutes. Allow to cool to room temperature.

Combine the blueberry mixture with the raspberries and yogurt in a food processor or blender and process until smooth. Refrigerate until thoroughly chilled, about 3 hours.

MAKES 6 SERVINGS

Nutritional information per serving

144 calories ▾ 0.6 grams of fat

PEACH SMOOTHIE SOUP

▼ ▼

1¾ cups granulated sugar

1 cup water

6 ripe peaches, peeled, pitted, and cut into quarters

1 tablespoon fresh lemon juice

*T*his soup captures the essence of fresh, ripe peaches. Make sure the peaches are ripe. To peel the peaches, drop them into briskly boiling water; one minute in the water and the skins should slip right off.

▼ ▼ ▼

Combine the sugar and water in a small heavy saucepan and place over low heat. Stir until the sugar is dissolved. Increase the heat to medium-high and boil the mixture just until the syrup is clear, 2 to 3 minutes. Remove from the heat and cool to room temperature. (The sugar syrup can be used at this point or it can be refrigerated for up to a month for later use.)

Place the peaches in a food processor or blender with 1 cup of the sugar syrup and the lemon juice and process until smooth. Refrigerate until thoroughly chilled. Ladle into chilled bowls to serve.

MAKES 6 SERVINGS
Nutritional information per serving
262 calories ▾ 0.1 grams of fat

TANGY STRAWBERRY RHUBARB SOUP

▼ ▼

1 pound rhubarb, ends trimmed
  and cut into 2-inch pieces

½ cup granulated sugar

¼ cup cold water

1 quart fresh strawberries,
  rinsed, hulled, and sliced

1 pint nonfat vanilla frozen
  yogurt

This is a thick soup with a sharp, not-too-sweet flavor. The rhubarb is cooked just until it's tender. Off the heat, the strawberries are stirred in, which cooks them only slightly, leaving them plump, red, and still juicy. Serve this soup over vanilla frozen yogurt for a spectacular dessert.

▼ ▼ ▼

Combine the rhubarb with the sugar and water in a heavy 4-quart saucepan, preferably one with a nonstick surface, and place over medium-high heat. Stir until the sugar is dissolved and the liquid is simmering. Reduce the heat to medium-low and continue cooking until the rhubarb is soft, about 15 minutes. Remove from the heat. Add the strawberries, reserving 12 slices to use as a garnish, and stir well to combine. Transfer the mixture to a large mixing bowl, allow to come to room temperature, cover and refrigerate until thoroughly chilled.

To serve, place a scoop of vanilla frozen yogurt into individual serving bowls. Top each serving with about 1 cup of the strawberry rhubarb soup. Garnish with the reserved sliced strawberries.

MAKES 6 SERVINGS
Nutritional information per serving
164 calories ▾ 0.5 grams of fat

TROPICAL FRUIT SOUP

▼ ▼

1¾ cups granulated sugar

1 cup water

2 tablespoons fresh lemon juice

½ pound kumquats, stems removed, seeded, and very thinly sliced

Juice and finely chopped zest of 1 lime

1 cup green seedless grapes, thinly sliced

1 small ripe mango, peeled, pitted, and finely chopped

1 small ripe papaya, peeled, seeded, and finely chopped

1 star fruit, thinly sliced

*A*n exotic soup that will delight and surprise. The base of the soup is a very sweet sugar syrup, but the combination of fresh tropical fruits with their tangy, puckery flavors balances the sweetness.

▼   ▼   ▼

Combine the sugar, water, and lemon juice in a small heavy saucepan and place over medium-high heat. When the mixture boils, stir once or twice and allow to boil until the mixture turns clear, 2 to 3 minutes. Remove from the heat. Transfer the sugar syrup to a mixing bowl and stir in the sliced kumquats. Refrigerate until thoroughly chilled, at least 2 hours. Stir in the lime juice.

Pour ⅓ cup of the sugar syrup into each of six individual soup plates. Divide the kumquats among the servings. To each serving add some of the grapes, 2 tablespoons each of the mango and papaya, and 2 or 3 slices of the star fruit. Garnish each serving with some of the chopped lime zest.

MAKES 6 SERVINGS
Nutritional information per serving
310 calories ▾ 0.4 grams of fat

PEAR AND RED WINE SOUP

▼ ▼

½ cup granulated sugar

2 cups dry red wine, such as
  Merlot or Chianti

2 cups water

6 pears, preferably Bosc,
  peeled, cored, and cut into
  sixths lengthwise

Zest of 1 lemon, cut into fine
  julienne strips

*T*his is one of my favorite winter desserts. The pears are infused with an intense, rich flavor and a deep mahogany color that comes from the red wine. You can use any type of pear, as long as it's ripe, but my preference is for Bosc pears because even when they're ripe, they are easy to peel and they hold up to cooking without falling apart.

▼   ▼   ▼

Combine the sugar, wine, and water in a heavy 4-quart saucepan over medium heat and stir until the sugar dissolves. Add the pears and bring to a simmer. Reduce the heat to medium-low, cover, and cook until the pears are a deep mahogany color, tender when pierced with a sharp knife, and the liquid has reduced by about half, 25 to 30 minutes. Remove from the heat and cool to room temperature. Refrigerate several hours or overnight until thoroughly chilled. Ladle the pear soup into dessert bowls and garnish each serving with some of the lemon zest.

MAKES 6 SERVINGS
Nutritional information per serving
219 calories ▾ 0.7 grams of fat

LE DÔME'S STRAWBERRY SOUP

▼ ▼

3 pints fresh strawberries,
rinsed, hulled, and cut in half
or quarters lengthwise
¼ cup granulated sugar

I tasted this soup in a Paris bistro called Le Dôme. The recipe is incredibly simple; the results depend on really ripe, flavorful, and fragrant strawberries.

▼ ▼ ▼

Combine 1 pint of the strawberries with the sugar in a food processor or blender and process until smooth. Scrape down the sides of the workbowl and continue processing until the mixture is completely pureed.

Place the remaining 2 pints of strawberries in a medium-size mixing bowl and pour the strawberry-and-sugar mixture over them. Stir well to combine. Refrigerate at least 1 hour, or up to 3 hours, until ready to serve.

MAKES 6 SERVINGS
Nutritional information per serving
75 calories ▼ 0.5 grams of fat

INDEX